ALSO BY JOHN GIERACH

Fool's Paradise
Still Life with Brook Trout
At the Grave of the Unknown Fisherman
Death, Taxes, and Leaky Waders
Standing in a River Waving a Stick
Fishing Bamboo
Another Lousy Day in Paradise
Dances with Trout
Even Brook Trout Get the Blues
Where the Trout Are All as Long as Your Leg
Sex, Death, and Fly-Fishing
Fly-fishing Small Streams
The View from Rat Lake
Trout Bum
Fly-fishing the High Country

NO SHORTAGE OF GOOD DAYS

JOHN GIERACH

Simon & Schuster
New York   London   Toronto   Sydney

Simon & Schuster
1230 Avenue of the Americas
New York, NY 10020

First Simon & Schuster hardcover edition May 2011

SIMON & SCHUSTER and colophon are registered trademarks
of Simon & Schuster, Inc.

For information about special discounts for bulk purchases,
please contact Simon & Schuster Special Sales at
1-866-506-1949 or business@simonandschuster.com.

The Simon & Schuster Speakers Bureau can bring authors
to your live event. For more information or to book an event,
contact the Simon & Schuster Speakers Bureau at
1-866-248-3049 or visit our website at www.simonspeakers.com.

Designed by Akasha Archer

Manufactured in the United States of America

10   9   8   7   6   5   4   3   2   1

Library of Congress Cataloging-in-Publication Data

Gierach, John, date.
    No shortage of good days / by John Gierach; illustrations by Glen Wolff.
       p.   cm.
       1. Fly fishing—Anecdotes. I. Title.
SH456.G576   2011
799.12'4—dc22   2010043739
ISBN 978-0-7432-9175-0
ISBN 978-1-4516-1011-6 (ebook)

Everything outside was elegant and savage and fleshy. Everything inside was slow and cool and vacant. It seemed a shame to stay inside.

—JOHN CHEEVER

CONTENTS

NO SHORTAGE
OF GOOD DAYS

1

THIRD-RATE TROUT STREAMS

It's always good to get home after a long road trip, but it sometimes takes a specific act of will to *go* home. That's why the drive back is so often passed in the kind of anticlimactic silence that descends when there's simply nothing left to say. It's not that you could—or would—spend the rest of your days standing in cold water swatting deer flies, it's just that the detritus of daily life has been piling up while you were gone, and by contrast traveling and fishing seem so, you know . . . uncomplicated.

Doug Powell, Vince Zounek, and I had been down in the San Juan Mountains in southwestern Colorado: a 10,000-square-mile landscape (bigger than Vermont) where ancient, erosion-resistant crystalline rock is uplifted to elevations up to 14,000 feet, a dozen rivers have at least some of their headwaters, and where, as Jeff Rennicke said, "horizons stack up like cord wood."

We were on the first leg of a trip to scout some obscure mountain creeks, following a haphazard collection of tips. Some of these came from dependable fishing friends and were solid gold. Suggestions from strangers involved a little more blind faith—especially when there was a long hike in the deal—but when you hear about the same creek in the same hushed tones from two or three fishermen, you begin to hope there's something to it.

We were specifically looking for the kind of small creeks that many fishermen consider to be third-rate and not worth the trouble. It's not that these things are never fished or that they're a sure bet, and in fact some of them really *aren't* worth the trouble. It's just that they're ignored out of hand by some, and the remaining fishing pressure is diluted by the sheer number of streams and the scale of the region, so there's still some good, overlooked water.

We'd collected these hints and rumors over the last few seasons, and when we plotted them all together on a map at home, they revealed a big loop south through the San Juans, followed by a meandering course back north along the West Slope in the general direction of home. But beyond the logistics, I'm not sure where the idea for this trip came from. (As usual, we talked a lot about where we'd go, but never about *why*.) I do know we all like small mountain streams for their peace, quiet, and seclusion and for their homeliness set in drop-dead gorgeous surroundings. The countless feeder creeks in the Mountain West are like dogs: genetically identical and often nothing special, but still unique and lovable.

And I, for one, have this idea that constant exposure to the ordinary is good for the soul. I *have* met some high-brow fishermen who bragged that they only fished at the best places with the best guides at the best times of year and who claimed to not only always catch fish, but to always catch lots of real big ones. If true, a life without drama must be awfully boring, and if false—as you have to suspect—then lugging around an ego that requires that much preening must be a terrible burden. In the end, the best fishermen I know have all finally developed a kind of professional polish without losing the hopeless goofiness of the beginner. You could say the same thing about fishing that they say about baseball: that it takes an adult to play the game well, but it takes a kid to think it's important.

The plan was to stay the first few nights in the ski resort town of Telluride at a "pretty nice place" where Doug had gotten an off-season comp through the ski magazine he works for. I'd never been to this tourist town, but Doug had contacts there and it was smack in the middle of some of the streams we wanted to explore, so I figured it would be fine.

I didn't think about it again until we pulled up to the portico of a place that looked a little like pictures I'd seen of Windsor Castle: the poshest hotel in a town that makes a fetish out of being posh. I assumed this was another one of Doug's deadpan jokes—that we'd all have a good laugh and then drive a few blocks to a regular old motel—but the joke was, this is actually where we'd be staying.

There were the briefest sidelong glances from the doorman and the lady at the front desk, but Colorado is a blessedly casual place with no discernible dress code, and in hotels of this caliber they don't care if you're an eccentric CEO, a minor character actor going native, or just what you appear to be. The assumption is that if you're there, you must *belong* there.

I naturally had some favorites among the creeks we fished over the next few days. There were no trails along the two forks of the stream with a Spanish name—always a promising sign—and they were both narrow and brush-choked enough that in most places we had to wade up the middle of the shallow channel, taking turns on the pools.

The east fork flowed down a steep valley lined with alpine crags jutting above rolling tundra that looked like a lumpy green mattress. We caught brown trout, rainbows, and some brookies from fingerling size up to twelve and thirteen inches, plus one brown Doug got that we guessed at sixteen inches. The occasional big fish from a little freestone stream is often old and worn out, with a skinny body and a big head, but this guy was as sleek as a spring creek fish: a truly astonishing trout from a stream you can cross almost anywhere without getting in over your knees. Vince and I kidded Doug about taking so long to land the fish until we saw it, at which point things became quietly serious for a couple of minutes. We were traveling light and hadn't expected anything like this, so no one had a landing net.

An old skiing friend of Vince's who now lives in the area took us to a stretch of the west fork in a narrow, forested canyon. He put us in at an unlikely-looking place we'd never have picked on our own and pointed out the deep cliff pool where, earlier that year, well after sunset, he'd landed a trout he guessed at twenty inches long.

"What was it?" I asked. "Brown? Cutthroat?"

"Don't know," he replied. "Like I said, it was dark and I didn't have a flashlight."

This is the kind of authentic-sounding detail that marks a true fish story, an unusually skilled storyteller or, in rare cases, both.

We caught medium-sized cutthroats and brook trout on dry flies until late afternoon, when Vince's friend took us ten miles down the drainage to a stretch of private water he had access to. It was on the same stream, but that far down the valley, it flowed more slowly and was lined with cottonwoods instead of pine and spruce. It was also wider and more open and winding, with long runs and deep undercuts on the outside bends: more what you think of as classic trout water. The guy had meant this as a treat for his old friend and his two partners and we appreciated it, but although we did okay, I was not so secretly pleased that the public stretch upstream in the national forest had been better.

We fished on into the evening, when the air temperature finally dropped enough to put off the deer flies, which was a relief. They'd been bad for the last couple of days, and although you do get used to them, there are times when you can't help hating them deeply, both as a species and as individuals. Deer flies are insanely persistent, they bite like miniature wolverines, sometimes drawing blood, and slathering yourself with bug dope has about the same effect on them as pouring syrup on a pancake. Their only advantage is that they're slow, so you can stop now and then and kill a few out of pure revenge.

I wish I'd bothered to count the other fishermen we saw in these mountains so I could impress you with how few there were. (This area is world-famous among skiers, but although it's laced with hundreds of miles of pretty little trout streams, it doesn't seem to be a big destination for fly fishers.) The point is, we had every place we fished to ourselves. That's not just pleasant; it's also crucial in this kind of fishing, since anyone working up a small creek ahead of you will catch some fish, spook the rest and blow the fishing for anywhere from a few hours to the rest of the day.

As it turned out, the fishing in most places was better than we'd hoped, although, as I said, we'd been handed most of this on what amounted to a silver platter, so we could really only congratulate ourselves on our ability to follow directions. But then one of the things you eventually learn as a fisherman is how to accept luck and generosity as if you deserved both.

Of course, there was always a slight disconnect when we'd get off the water, take off our wading boots, and drive back to Telluride. It was raining lightly one evening when we got back to Windsor Castle, so we stashed our gear in our rooms and put on rain slickers to walk the few blocks into town for dinner. We'd barely gotten to the end of the driveway when the concierge trotted up holding an umbrella and said if we'd wait a minute, he'd have the limousine brought around to take us wherever we wanted to go. We said thanks, but no thanks; we'd rather walk. We were heading to a cheap sandwich shop we'd found where the nearly invisible working class hung out, and arriving in a chauffeur-driven limo would have blown our populist cover.

This was the same concierge who, when he learned we were fishing, offered to arrange for a guide. When Vince told him we were so good we didn't *need* a guide, he'd said, "Of course, sir." Was he joshing us back dryly, or being obsequious? There was no way to tell.

There was only one stream that we thought might have

fished a little better on a different day. It was just under a hundred road miles north of the San Juans in the aptly named Ragged Mountains. The stream was named for a nearby mineral deposit and flowed out of a dark canyon with sheer thousand-foot cliffs that seemed to lean in farther the longer you stared up at them, finally inducing something between vertigo and claustrophobia and making you look away.

We did manage to get a few rainbows and cutthroats—fat, healthy little sausages that glistened even in the shade—but only a few, so we took to fishing a stretch for half an hour or so before busting upstream on a faint trail to try it farther along. We'd been told by our source to "go on up in there a ways," which seemed straightforward enough until we began to wonder how far "a ways" might be. This was a long stream with the access at the bottom of the canyon that we'd used and another far upstream off a pass. But day-trip range from either end would still leave several miles in the middle that you could fish only from an overnight camp, and for all we knew that's what the guy meant.

We turned around with enough daylight left that we wouldn't have to try to follow the trail down the canyon in the dark and spent most of the walk out planning a return trip. For some reason, it's the streams that look good but don't show off on the first try that get under your skin. A second day with an earlier start was a possibility, but we had other places we wanted to try, and ever since we'd left our snazzy digs in Telluride, we'd been relieved to be on the move again.

Then the conversation drifted on to some other streams we might go back to sometime and then, inevitably, to other new creeks and rivers we'd only heard about. At a place where the trail threaded through a dense stand of scrub oak, we came on a steaming-fresh bear turd and felt the usual tingle of ambivalence. Everyone loves bears, and when there's one around, you always want to see it, but maybe not at close range in such tight quarters.

My fondest memory is of another little creek that was named after its own water chemistry. By then we were back in vaguely familiar territory and at that point you reach in any trip where it's hard to tell if things are building to a crescendo or beginning to wind down. A sure sign of the latter is when someone breaks the spell by uttering that chilling sentence that begins, "You know, as soon as we get home I'm gonna have to . . ." But that hadn't happened yet, so we were still okay.

At the one-lane wooden bridge where the stream passed under a dirt road, it didn't look like much more than a trickle running through a bog: the kind of thing most fishermen would glance at without even slowing down. We checked our directions again, thinking we could be in the wrong place, but no, this had to be it. One of my oldest and most trusted friends had told us to try this, and it was only the memory of his raised eyebrows and conspiratorial grin that kept us from shrugging and driving away.

The story here was that this little creek was a happy accident of water chemistry, hidden in plain sight, and a little hard to get on because the easy access was blocked by private land. From its confluence with a larger stream on up to where a rich spring-fed creek poured in—not much more than half a mile—the improbably fertile water grew fish food by the ton. There were brown trout and a few rainbows that you'd be happy to catch anywhere, let alone from an obscure little creek that you need a detailed map just to find. Never mind exactly how big some of these trout were. We hardly believed it ourselves, so why would you?

Lower down, around the first couple of bends, there were a few miniature clearings blanketed in cow parsnip and leafy aster, but the creek quickly went into a narrow lane of dense willow and river birch where the known world consisted solely of brush and water, fat, eager trout, and 50,000 biting flies. There weren't many rises, but some medium-sized tan caddis were popping off sporadically and the fish would happily go for a well-placed dry fly.

There was an all-too-short stretch of some of the best small stream water I've ever seen anywhere. Then we passed the confluence with the spring creek, which flowed out of private land. We peeked up it anyway. It was clear as glass and matted with duckweed and watercress, but from there on up, both forks of the creek were too small to be anything but nursery water for baby trout.

This was clearly the end of it, but we slogged on up the main branch anyway. It was a continuous ankle-deep riffle, and the brush grew together over the water to form a low ceiling. For the next few hundred yards, there was no holding water and no room to cast if there had been. By the time we gave up, it was raining, we were all but crawling up the stream bed, the deer flies seemed downright giddy about finding fresh meat under such thin skin, and the effort was finally beginning to seem pointless. On a trip where the whole idea was to go far enough, it was inevitable that we'd eventually go *too* far.

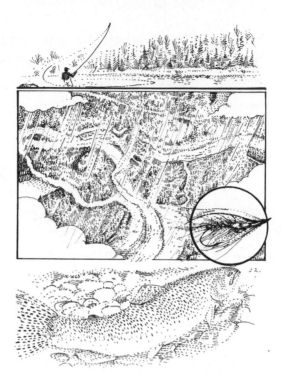

2

SKAGIT

There are plenty of stories about not catching steelhead, so why tell another? Maybe because fishermen have always been prouder of their successes than they deserve to be, but also more haunted by their failures. Or because the unlikelihood of catching these fish defines the sport and makes those who practice it seem mildly insane. Many steelheaders—especially the younger ones—embrace the label, but they really *aren't* insane. They've simply developed an acquired taste, like sashimi

11

or okra, and have somehow combined the hyperactivity of the fanatic with the glacial patience it takes to cast for weeks without much encouragement from the fish.

It was late April when Vince and I flew out to coastal Washington State to fish the Skagit River and one of its major tributaries, the Sauk. This was new water for both of us, so we spent the first three days floating with guides to get the lay of the land and the rest of the time on foot on our own. It was our usual attempt to achieve the best of both worlds—expert advice and self-reliant solitude—as well as to save a few bucks on the trip.

All rivers have something to recommend them if you look hard enough, but the Skagit is a landmark. Famous steelheaders cut their teeth on the river, and there are fly patterns and a style of spey casting named after it. Also, a steelhead bum I know—a young guy with no permanent address and no visible means of support—told me the last time he breezed through town that it was demanding as hell but worth the effort, with a run of the biggest, wildest and otherwise coolest steelhead south of central British Columbia. Greg Thomas once described these fish as a race of "exquisitely proportioned native steelhead" that stay at sea longer than most and that can reach weights of twenty pounds or more.

Okay, but then the flip side is that there aren't that many of these outstanding fish left. Historically, steelhead runs in the Skagit are estimated to have been in the neighborhood of 30,000 fish, while today it's closer to a piddling 2,000. The main culprits are the usual suspects for the region: offshore pollution, commercial fishing, and erosion from clear-cut logging that flushes the river with mud after every rain, bumping the flows unnaturally and clogging the spawning gravel with silt.

Fishing is with barbless hooks only, and all wild steelhead in the Skagit and Sauk must be released. Furthermore, it's now illegal anywhere in the state of Washington even to lift a caught wild steelhead from the water, making the standard grip-and-grin snapshot a misdemeanor. Puget Sound steelhead have now been placed on the endangered species list. That's probably a wise move, if not exactly a good sign.

These minor, stopgap measures are unquestionably necessary, and incidentally much easier than cleaning up the world's oceans and scaling the commercial fishing and lumber industries back to sustainable levels. But you wonder how much good they can do, since by the time steelhead return to their home rivers, the damage has already been done. If trout are indicator species for the health of a single stream, then steelhead are indicators for a hemisphere and any real solution has to be as nearly global as the problem.

That's not an obituary for the river, it's just what steelhead fishers are up against now in too many drainages: the hope of occasionally glimpsing something that was once commonplace and is now rare. You could wish you'd been there fifty years ago, but you weren't, and regret is pointless. The fact is, if you have a certain kind of quixotic temperament, steelhead can still be too compelling to ignore, and although there may be only a slim chance of success, the inescapable fact is that you'll never catch one if you stay home.

I've managed to go steelheading only twice a year at best since I took it up six or seven years ago, and at that rate I'm probably fated to be a perpetual dilettante, but I've nonetheless evolved into a kind of low-level fanatic. I usually come to my senses when I get home, but at least while I'm doing it, there's the notion that real fishing is steelhead fishing, while everything else is just a pastime.

Vince and I rented a car at the Seattle airport, drove north along the coast, and got a room at a motel in a small town not far from the river. This was a typically characterless American burg beside an interstate comprised of cookie-cutter housing developments, strip malls, and burger joints: everything quick, cheap, and temporary in the interest of hyperconsumerism. If not for the dank northwestern spring weather and some telltale western red cedars, it could have been a suburb of Toledo, but then it was just a place to shower and sleep between days on the water.

Early the next morning, we met Dave McCoy with Emerald Water Anglers out of Seattle to do a float that put in on the Sauk and took out on the Skagit. Over the next two days, we fished parts of both rivers with two other guides from the same outfit, Ryan Smith and Dylan Rose—picking each of their brains for road and foot access to good pools for later. These guys were all young and competent and as different from each other as we all tend to be, but still with the weirdly similar stories most guides share. These involve hard, seasonal work, mediocre pay, and a good life outside—at least for the time being. (You'll hear that it's unfair to define a person by the work he does, but I've always thought that was first said by someone who didn't like their job.) Living close to the bone in order to do something you love seems more difficult now than it used to be, but then it was hard enough when I did it, too. I was just too young to care, which is probably still the secret.

I got my only hit of the trip on that first day: just a little tweak at the end of a long swing somewhere on the lower Sauk.

I know you're supposed to feed a steelhead the loop of loose line you're holding under the index finger of your rod hand before you set, allowing the fish to turn and take the hook in the corner of its mouth. I *know* that, but nearly forty years of trout fishing has imprinted the idea that one jerk should immediately be followed by another, and instinct always trumps intelligence. In other words, I fucked it up.

Dave said it's best to get a strike later in a trip, when you're half asleep from days of casting and the fish pulls the loop straight before you can react. It occurred to me that all the steelhead I'd caught had been in exactly that situation or, rarely, when I knew a fish was there and was ready for it.

I said, "Well, it was probably just a sea-run cutthroat anyway."

Dave said, "Oh, I don't think so."

There'd been hard rains recently, but the Skagit was still in good shape, and although the Sauk was a little high and slightly off-color, it was dropping and clearing, which is exactly what you want it to do. The weather was auspicious (chilly, cloudy, and drizzly), and the run was supposed to be nearing its height as the season wound to a close at the end of April. Word around the river was that not many steelhead were being caught, but that was the kind of thing that could, and should, turn around at any moment. So we fell into the usual persistent drill of going from one good run to another with the guides, fishing it methodically and then moving on to the next: covering water at a steady pace designed for the long haul. After a few fishless days, this begins to look suspiciously like work, but in a way that's hard to put your finger on, it's not.

Both the Sauk and the Skagit are big, wide rivers with lots of long, luxurious runs that are exactly what steelhead like, that is, water three to six feet deep with a rubble rock bottom and walking-speed current. Almost everyone here uses a two-handed rod because even a beginner, once he's worked out the first annoying kinks, can get a longer cast with less effort using a spey rod than he can with a single-hander. I'm thinking especially of a huge pool called the Mixer, where the flows of the Skagit and Sauk combine and where even a tournament caster would come up short.

There's an element of endurance to this technique that casting instructors seldom mention. With periodic breaks to move from one run to another, stop for lunch, and such, you can end up casting for ten hours a day, day after day. The best advice I've heard so far was that you should work out the longest cast you can possibly make, then reel in ten or fifteen feet of line and fish that. Otherwise, you'll beat yourself up.

It *is* possible to catch steelhead by simply going through the motions (I've done it), but the best fishermen have definite ideas about the day-to-day nuts and bolts of it as well as some more esoteric theories.

Fishing guide Mark Bachmann from Oregon thinks you should maintain the exact same interval of time between casts as you work your way down a run, because a steelhead will see the fly two or even three casts away, coming closer with each swing, and begin to anticipate it. But if he has to wait too long or the intervals are uneven, he'll quickly lose interest. I mean, he *is* only a fish.

I heard secondhand about a guy who thinks steelhead are repelled by the electromagnetic fields generated by power lines, so he fishes especially long and hard below the places where they cross rivers, thinking the fish will be stacked up there.

Another steelheader once told me that he always wants to be the second or even the third guy to fish a run. He thinks the first fisherman or two get the fish curious or agitated enough that when he finally comes along, they'll be ready to bite.

I met a man on the Salmon River in Idaho who had only ever fished one fly for steelhead: a medium-sized orange streamer. He said it must be a good pattern because he caught all his fish on it.

But for the most part, the best steelheaders simply understand where the fish will be under various conditions—at least in a general way—and are able both to spot those places and to put good casts to them. They'll probably have some well-considered theories about steelhead behavior, presentation, and fly patterns, but, more important, they can make a fly swim properly and get it to the right depth with different sinking heads, creative mending, or both. Some are impressive casters; others are simply accurate and persistent, and of course the best are in touch with something rare, instinctive, and possibly ancient that the rest of us only glimpse by accident from time to time. And if it seems like magic, who's to say it's not?

One day while floating with Dylan Rose, we drifted past a thin, gray-haired fisherman wading the Sauk, and Dylan said, reverently, "That's Harry Lemire." Lemire is a legendary steelheader and fly tier who has fished the region since the late 1950s. In his book *Steelhead Fly Fishing*, Trey Combs described him as the rare fisherman who became famous simply by virtue of being good. "He does not write, make videos, operate a fly-fishing store, guide, or otherwise commercially indulge his love for the sport," Combs wrote. It's been said that on especially good days of fishing, he'll cut the point off his hook because he likes to see the fish jump, but doesn't want to catch too many of them. That story alone makes him the fly-fishing equivalent of a Zen master.

As we drifted on past, Dylan said, "There's a guy who's caught more steelhead on this river than anyone alive, and look at him: He's wading calf-deep and fishing forty feet of line on a one-handed rod." He didn't have to add that everyone else on the river was wading to his waist and casting twice that far with a two-hander, covering as much water as possible as a substitute for actually knowing where the fish will be. You could see the gears turning as Dylan scoped out the unimpressive little run Harry was fishing and noted its location.

So we fished; first with the guides and then later on our own, driving county roads and trying to decipher the directions I'd scribbled in a moving boat in the kind of steady drizzle that wrinkles the notebook pages and makes the ink bleed. The weather was far from awful—just gray, wet, and chilly—but over time we began to feel soggy and beat-up anyway. The thermos of coffee—whether it was under the seat in the boat or back in the car—became more iconic than usual. You'd want to ration it carefully so it would last, but you'd also want to drink it all before it got cold. Two-thirds of the way down a two-hundred-yard run, it was possible to worry more about the temperature of your coffee than about whether or not there'd be a steelhead lying at the tailout.

To serious coffee drinkers like Vince and me, being in Washington State was like dying and going to heaven. There was good coffee everywhere, even at gas stations, and if you suddenly needed a fresh cup, you rarely had to drive more than a mile before you'd come upon a little kiosk where you could drive up and get whatever you wanted without getting out of the car and where the young barista would always ask, "How's the fishing?" You got the sense that even on the loneliest stretch of river you could yell out an order for a double Americano with cream and someone would bring it to you.

The weather stayed cold and foggy, sometimes clearing enough for the snowcapped peaks of the Cascades to peek out for half an hour at a time, but never quite enough for the weak sun to cast an actual shadow. (Steelhead are supposed to like gray weather.) It kept drizzling, but the heavy rains held off and the Sauk continued to drop and clear. (Steelhead are supposed to like water that's dropping and clearing.) You couldn't exactly say the rivers were full of steelhead, but things were looking as good as they could look under the circumstances.

One day, while fishing down a long run, we saw a sport with a guide land a steelhead on a spinning rod across the river. As per the regulations, they didn't lift it out of the water, but from my vantage point I guessed it at around fifteen pounds. The fisherman seemed weirdly unconcerned, but the guide threw his fists in the air, turned his face to the sky and yelled, "Yes!" I love an enthusiastic guide, but this may also have been a sign that he hadn't seen a lot of fish recently.

After that, Vince and I both stopped and changed flies, if only for something to do. This is especially tempting for me because I tend to tie more steelhead flies than I need as a security blanket. I have a few that I've actually caught fish on, and many more that someone recommended or that I just thought were pretty. For this trip I'd painstakingly tied some Skagit Mists, a lovely but complicated Dec Hogan spey pattern. When we'd talked on the phone before the trip, Dave had said this was a good fly for the Skagit but that he didn't use it himself because it was too difficult and time-consuming to tie. To a certain kind of fly tier (adequate, but with delusions of grandeur), that was like waving a red flag at a bull.

Still, I've noticed that the less it matters which fly you use, the longer you'll stare into your fly box waiting for inspiration, and when you ask a guide or a more experienced steelheader his opinion of any pattern, he's likely to shrug and say, "What the hell, try it." Which is to say, this is not an exact science.

Hope does eventually begin to fade when you're steelheading, but it never entirely goes away. A friend of mine caught the biggest steelhead of his life literally on his last cast of an otherwise fishless weeklong trip. At the end of that final day, his guide said, "All right, that's it. We gotta go." My friend said, "Okay, I'll just fish out this cast."

So you fish well right to the bitter end, telling yourself, truthfully, that how well you do something is probably more important than why you do it. If you have the disposition for it, this is a better way than most to spend your time, even if you never hook that wild twenty-pound steelhead. You'll hear fishermen talk about being humbled by a river and we all know what that means and how it feels, but somehow the language of competition doesn't quite ring true. It's not so much that the river beats you; it's more that the river doesn't even know you're there.

3

HOME WATER

I sometimes wonder why I have this passing affection for the North Platte River in Wyoming, especially the hard-used stretch from Gray Reef Dam down to Casper. I don't spend a lot of time there, but most years I float it with friends early and late in the season: a couple of times in April and maybe once or twice in October or even November if the weather holds. The streamer fishing can be good then, and there's at least a chance that the ubiquitous crowd will be a little thinner than usual.

This *is* a good trout river, and although it's a five-hour drive from home, it's still the nearest river that's big enough to float in a drift boat, which is part of its attraction. It also has some long, wide runs that are custom-made for a streamer fished with a two-handed spey rod. One of my goals is to become a proficient spey caster, but there are very few rivers in this part of the West that are large enough to practice on.

But then there are some other things I *don't* like about it. This stretch of the North Platte is a pretty river flowing through high plains sagebrush country punctuated by groves of cottonwoods and impressive cliffs, but it's also kind of junky. The normal residue of the working ranches along the river is one thing—people are trying to make a living here and they can't always be neat about it—but in public spots where you can drive in to the river or where people regularly beach their boats to wade fish, there are shameful piles of trash.

Now and then, you'll find the box a spinning reel came in or a godawful tangle of monofilament, but mostly it's the typical American effluvium of pop cans, beer bottles, pizza boxes, Big Mac wrappers, and such. (This gives me hope that some of the junk comes from partying teenagers instead of fishermen, although that could just be wishful thinking.) In any case, all of this stuff could have easily been picked up and put back in the boat or car it arrived in—it just wasn't. There was a time when my friends and I tried to clean things up a little, but it became obvious that to make any kind of dent we'd need a second drift boat to serve as a garbage scow.

This is also a justifiably famous river that's close to the medium-sized city of Casper and not hard to get to (what recreation managers would call an "urban fishery"), so it's often crowded with conventional drift boats and those now-common one-man pontoon things. Most people observe the normal etiquette, but there are times when you can't help but float through the water someone else is fishing, or vice versa. If that happens two or three times a day, it's no big deal, but when it happens twenty or thirty times a day, everyone starts to feel a little cramped.

But to their credit, most people handle that graciously. Even on a day when you run into dozens of other fishermen, only one or two will be rude and grumpy. That's a pretty good average, and I've long since stopped taking that sort of thing personally. After all, everywhere you go as a tourist-fisherman is someone else's home water, and the regulars inevitably feel proprietary about it, although their real problem may be that even on a river with several strikes against it, they still expect every day of fishing to be perfect. Settling for second best is the kind of deadly habit that can ultimately leave you holding the muddy end of the stick, but at the same time, we all have to develop a definition of "good enough" that doesn't make us hate the world.

I've always been fascinated by fishermen's peculiar fondness for certain local water, and I mean my own as well as others. Sometimes it's so obvious it amounts to a cliché, like the lake at the old summer cabin or the secret honey hole where you always hike in by a different route so as not to wear a trail others might follow. But just as often, it's a spot that's too popular and crowded, too trashy, or a second-rate stream that you have a soft spot for in spite of the fish being small and far between.

By definition, home water is close to home, so at first it can seem like a compromise weighted heavily toward proximity. Most of us who write about fishing have gotten around to telling about the sad little neighborhood puddle we first fished as kids—for no other reason than that we couldn't be trusted to go any farther on our own. In most cases, this thing's only virtue was that it was permanently wet, but as poor as it was, it grabbed our attention, caused something to click, and turned us into lifelong fishermen—either right then or eventually.

Mine was a little warmwater brook in Illinois that was exactly five doors down from my grandmother's house, where I was born. It probably had a real name, but it was known locally as the Stink Creek because it smelled funny, although at the time I thought that was just how creeks smelled. Not too many miles upstream was one of those dreary midwestern industrial towns that even then was beginning to show signs of decay. This would have been a good twenty years before the establishment of the Environmental Protection Agency, so God only knows what was being openly dumped in the water. I used to get a persistent rash every summer and to this day my mother thinks it came from that creek, but at least the little bullheads that lived there weren't deformed—or at least no more deformed than a bull-head normally is.

A few years later, in the mid-1950s, my father got transferred and we moved to the relative paradise of Minnesota. The fish were bigger, prettier, and more numerous, the rash went away, and I learned that most of the lakes and rivers people fished in didn't have an odor that made your eyes water. But of course none of that made any real difference because I was already a fisherman.

We feel more in control when we begin to grow up, but whether we try to orchestrate our lives or just let things happen, most of us still just end up where we are in one way or another.

If we're fishermen, one of the first chores is to find the nearest water that holds fish. Life being what it is, we often don't get to choose our home water any more than we do our families.

I came out to the Rocky Mountains in the late 1960s more or less on purpose, but after years of randomly bouncing around, I just sort of ended up near a small foothills town in Colorado and some minor tributaries of the South Platte River. The streams were (and still are) lovely little things, but they weren't fished much back then because, in the grand scheme of fly fishing, they weren't considered to be very good. The town itself had one stoplight, two cafés, and was a place where fishing was understood and approved of, but it wasn't a full-blown fishing town full of visiting sports like, say, West Yellowstone, Montana. There wasn't even a fly shop, but you could buy flies, worms, and a fishing license at the hardware store.

I guess I was luckier than most in that regard, but there was still a time when I wistfully thought that if things had gone differently, my home water could have been something like the Henry's Fork in Idaho. I mean, things could be, and often *were* pretty loose in the sixties, so I could as easily have lit in one place as the other.

But then the more I fished these little creeks and the more I learned about them, the better I liked them. Part of that was just the constant exposure. Sure, there were better fisheries within a half day's drive—and I made those drives and other, longer ones often enough—but there was nowhere else where I could slip in an hour of fishing before work or two or three hours after and have a rod in my hand every day of the week.

The pangs of ambition still surfaced regularly, and now and then I'd get the thousand-yard stare thinking about bigger fish in more distant places. But then there's nothing like a little fish rising right in front of you to reestablish perspective, especially when you get two or three good drifts over him with what has to be the right fly and he still won't bite.

That's how it happens. It may begin as nothing more than a marriage of convenience, but most of us eventually end up falling for a nearby lake, stream, or pond that comes up short of the usual fly-fishing hype in some way. If you ask a fisherman who's traveled widely what his three or four favorite places are—and if he answers honestly—you'll probably be surprised by at least one of them.

Which is to say, your home water eventually gets under your skin and begins to define you as a fisherman. If nothing else, the skills it takes to fish it are the ones you use the most, so if you live on big water, you'll become a good distance caster out of necessity, while if you do most of your day-to-day fishing on small creeks like I do, you'll end up being deadly accurate at short ranges and a passably good stalker.

My old friend Ed Engle has a famous Colorado tailwater as his home river, so naturally he's become a top-notch match-the-hatch–style small fly fisherman, even to the point that he's written a couple of landmark books on the subject. I, on the other hand, am much more comfortable on freestone streams where the hatches are thin, the fish are hungry, and I can fish the same size 14 dry fly all season.

Beyond that, the place you fish the most affects your attitude about fly fishing. Some fishing trips are big adventures and we wouldn't have it any other way, but fishing your home water isn't exactly a special occasion. It's not that you don't care if you catch fish (if you didn't always care, you'd find a different sport), it's just that if you don't get some today, you can get them tomorrow or next week. You might even have one of those rare days when you go fishing, only to realize that for one reason or another, you shouldn't have gone fishing that day. This doesn't happen often, but it does happen, and it's not the end of the world. The final effect is that, over time, fly fishing ceases to be an isolated compartment of your life and becomes as ordinary as a cup of coffee or the evening news.

That's just good for the soul, but there are also specific benefits. For one thing, the largest part of fishing skill boils down to being supremely comfortable with a fly rod in your hand, and that only comes with practice. People who habitually fish their home water may or may not be what you'd call great fishermen, but they do tend to stay at the top of their game.

For another, fishing casually makes you more observant. With the pressure off, your attention wanders in the best way, so you notice things you wouldn't ordinarily see. Maybe these amount to lessons that help you catch more fish or invent a new fly pattern, or maybe they're just the small rewards you get for spending time outdoors. Either way, you learn to see what's there to be seen, and that will serve you well in the long run. I can say from experience that when you're far from home, the fish are big and the chips are down, you can get the kind of tunnel vision that will cause you to miss something crucial and obvious, but if you've already developed the habit of attentiveness, you're less likely to panic.

One of the first signs that you have home water is that a kind of simplicity creeps into the fishing you do there. You probably started out clanking around in the full vest and waders, but by now, through trial and error, you've pared things down to a single small fly box containing maybe a dozen patterns, plus clippers and a spare spool of tippet. You may also notice that you're catching more fish than you used to. This is a simple function of familiarity—you've learned where the fish will be, when they'll bite, and what they'll bite *on*—but the general idea of shedding superfluous baggage and doing better with less is something you may begin to ponder.

If you're one of those who keep a cheap rod and reel stashed in the car for emergencies (not exactly a throwaway, but not your best gear, either), you may eventually learn that the relative snazziness of your tackle doesn't have a whole lot to do with how well you fish. Something else to think about.

Fishing my home water also taught me that I'm as passionate and curious as anyone, but maybe not quite as driven as some. For instance, I found that on a slow day, a single fish against the odds could be plenty, while on an especially easy day, it became possible to stop at three or four trout, call it good, and then maybe go looking for a larger fish. Trying to scout up a big trout—even if it's only twelve inches long as opposed to the usual eight or nine—can mean more walking, looking, and thinking than actual fishing. I learned that in some situations, constant casting doesn't help a fisherman any more than aimlessly filling the air with lead would help a hunter.

I think the ideal home water is close enough to home that when you get the time and the wild hair to go fishing, you can be there before you start to have the second thoughts that are the curse of the aspiring deadbeat. Starting from my driveway, I can be on the stream stringing up a rod in six minutes (I timed it this morning), but that's just the closest place to fish, not the best. At the other extreme, I can drive for as long as forty-five minutes up into the national forest, and even if I have to hike for another hour to get where I want to be, I'll have my feet on the ground and a rod in my hand, so I'm fishing and all other bets are off. Any more travel time than that and my mind will start to wander, but those with more focused attention spans will have no trouble with a longer drive.

I think your home water should also be just good enough to hold your interest indefinitely, but not so good that it will ever draw much of a crowd. The actual parameters of that require-ment are up to the individual fisherman, but we'll each have our own minimum standard. I mean, at one time or another we've all been spotted using our best high-end tackle to try to catch a four-inch bluegill and felt a little like the village idiot fishing in a bucket.

My own level of sustained interest begins to fade when the average trout drops much below about eight inches—not to mention the possibility of an occasional whopper that could go thirteen or fourteen—and luckily that's what my home water gives up on the average day. On the other hand, maybe that's just what I've learned to settle for because it's what I have.

Everyone is different, but in my case I think it was for the best that my home water turned out to be modest. If I really *had* ended up on the banks of a world-famous and highly tech-nical river like the Henry's Fork, I'd have probably felt the need to become a local hotshot on a par with gurus like Mike Lawson and René Harrop. Chances are, I wouldn't have been up to it, and then where would I be?

As it is, I feel that I fish my local creeks as well as anyone and better than most, and although that may or may not be true, so few people care that I can go on believing it in peace. I've even reached the point where I can convincingly play the elder statesman with younger fishermen: telling them how the trout used to be bigger three and four decades ago and knowing that, since I was here then and they weren't, they're sort of forced to believe it.

I think the need for these places is genetically encoded, which is why we all had our secret spots as kids. At first it was behind the couch or under the bed, but eventually we got our legs under us and ventured outside. If we weren't lucky enough to have a patch of woods and a creek close by, there was at least an alley or a vacant lot or an unlandscaped corner of a friend's back yard that we could claim as our own because no one else was using it.

As adults, we still either have or subconsciously want what Carlos Castaneda called a "power spot" and Gerald Vizenor called a "panic hole": a quiet place where we can go for reasons that can be important or trivial but that are nonetheless private. For me it has to be at least marginally wild and have some fish in it, but even the longtime city dwellers I've known have had a secluded park bench, a spot on the back stairs of the art museum, or a corner table in an uncrowded coffee shop.

Are there drawbacks? That depends. A friend and I recently realized that making fly fishing a way of life instead of just a hobby (with the help of our respective home waters) has made us a couple of pretty one-dimensional characters. On the other hand, we agreed that we're two of the happiest people we know, albeit in a simple-minded sort of way.

Roughly along the same lines, being left alone to do something you love is a rare pleasure that's denied to many, but some are more suited to it than others. I won't get all New Age about this, but even if you're not your own best friend, you should still at least be able to stand your own company.

In my case, lots of solitude on my home water has trained me to be a low-key, persistent, and appreciative fisherman, but it has also made me too shy of crowds and noise to ever be comfortable in the twenty-first century. But then I've always had this tendency to go a little overboard. For most, there'll be more of a happy medium.

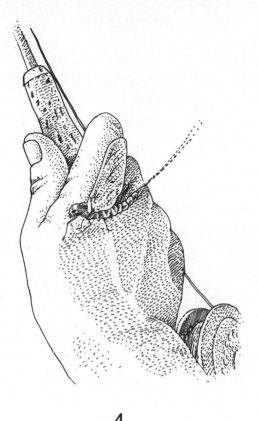

4

HEX

Paddling a canoe into an unfamiliar swamp at night in the company of two men you barely know is the kind of thing a fisherman does with only the slightest misgivings. After all, any of us who ever hire guides effectively put our safety into the hands of strangers and, if we're honest, we'll admit that even our own judgment is none too reliable at times. Still, I remembered what a friend once said about why he tries to stay out of cities. It seems that every time a voice comes out of a dark alley saying

"Psst, hey, come here a minute," he always goes. The point being that the line between having a little adventure and making a mistake can be a thin one.

I was fishing in northern Wisconsin with Bob White and guides Larry Mann and Wendy Williamson. We were there to fly-fish for smallmouth bass and muskies, and although there was also excellent trout fishing in the region, we'd planned to ignore it in favor of what to me are exotic fish. But then we learned that the Hexagenia mayfly hatch might still be on.

Now this wasn't just another mayfly hatch that we could have resisted. This was a nighttime emergence of the biggest mayflies in North America, just a hair shorter nose-to-tail than a calliope hummingbird. These things are large, juicy prey that hatch in the dark when fish feel safe, so they can bring those enormous brown trout that no one ever sees, but everyone believes in, to the surface to feed and, if everything goes right, to be caught on dry flies. Or at least so the story goes.

I did understand the pitfalls of this kind of temptation. We were already splitting our efforts between two species, and when there's too much to choose from, it's only human to spread yourself too thin, so that where you might have done one thing well, you end up doing two or three things poorly. I've succumbed to this tendency often enough to know how it can turn out and, frankly, fishing has been the least of it, so lately I've resolved to be one of those cool customers who diligently does what he came to do—or who "dances with who brung 'em," as we say out West—regardless of distractions. On the other hand, the happiest people I know are able to nicely split the difference between discipline and playfulness, so there's something to be said for staying loose.

I also knew that fishing that's supposed to be spectacular often isn't, if only because it's so rare to stumble into the complicated set of ideal conditions it takes for the best to happen. Or maybe it does turn out to be spectacular, but in a way other than you've been led to expect. Many fishing stories are really just about the beauty of the thing, but the language of the sport buries that theme in sub plots about fish size and numbers that amount to poetic license.

Years ago, I hit a salmon fly hatch in Canada totally by accident. (We were driving to a river in British Columbia and stopped to look at another river in Alberta out of curiosity.) The hatch wasn't what I'd expected, although at first I couldn't put my finger on what I thought was missing. In hindsight, it was just that I'd heard so many fantastic stories from so many wingnuts over the years that the reality couldn't possibly have lived up to the hype. I'd actually heard this hatch described as "life-changing," and when we finally drove over the pass into British Columbia two days later, I was almost disappointed to be the same old fisherman I'd been before, albeit one who'd just had a couple days of really fine dry-fly fishing. I suppose the real lesson was that I'd chased these elusive bugs off and on for decades through Colorado and Montana, only to stumble on them years after I'd given up, which must have something to do with the virtue of letting go of ambition.

Of course now, when I describe those two days to fishermen who've never experienced a salmon fly hatch, I speak from the great height of one who has and cryptically say it has to be seen to be believed. But it might actually be the other way around: maybe it has to be believed to be seen.

By the time I got a shot at the Hexagenia mayflies, I was a

few years older and had a firmer grip on my expectations about legendary hatches. I figured if all went well, some fish would be caught, maybe even some big ones, but it was really more a matter of curiosity, like finally stopping at a tourist trap in Kansas to see "The World's Largest Prairie Dog" after driving past the sign a dozen times in the last ten years. Those days of fishing that will make you smile on your deathbed do happen, but so far I've never seen any of them coming on the way to the river and only a few have had anything to do with so-called "super hatches." This was just an event I'd always wanted to see—if "see" is the right word for something that happens in the dark.

So we started asking around and learned that if we'd come in that same week anytime in the last ten or fifteen years, we'd have hit the three-week-long hatch right in the middle. But that season the bugs came off early because of unseasonably warm weather, so the hatch was either over or very near the end, depending on whom you asked. But then Larry hooked us up with Jim and Ken Harrold, two night-fishing brothers who thought it might still be coming off on an unnamed river an hour and a half's drive from where we were staying. They generously offered to take us there and were waiting at the fly shop the next evening when we got off the river.

I met Ken for the first time that night, but I'd talked to Jim briefly the year before. The only substantive thing we knew about each other was that we were both fishermen and that we shared a soft spot for bamboo fly rods. The bamboo angle was huge—it's a subculture within a subculture that really should have its own secret handshake—but still, as you drive off into the evening to an undisclosed location, an internal voice says, Okay, but really, who the hell *are* these guys?

An hour and a half later we parked at a two-lane bridge over a modest-sized, slow-moving river, unloaded Jim and Ken's two canoes, and stashed our gear on board. Then we stood around for half an hour talking quietly with a handful of mostly middle-aged men wearing headlamps, all of whom seemed to know each other. It was a warm June evening: a little humid, a little buggy, with a high overcast and not a breath of wind. There was no traffic on the two-lane road, and the only electric light was a mercury vapor lamp in a barnyard a quarter mile away. From that same direction, we could hear a dog barking in a tone of voice that suggested boredom.

The talk was what you'd expect: where everyone had been fishing recently, where they planned to fish next, and how tonight's stream flow, water clarity, and weather might affect the hatch, as if we weren't all about to find out. There was some anticipation but no hurry. The hatch would either come off or not, but it was just dusk, and nothing would happen until well after dark.

When I was a boy in the Midwest—not far from where I was standing, come to think of it; just a few hours' drive to the west in Minnesota—the common wisdom was that night fishing was sort of a shady business. It was perfectly legal, but there was still the suspicion that night fishers worked under the cover of darkness for the same reason burglars did, while God-fearing folk were at home watching *The Ed Sullivan Show*. Later, I fell in with some people who bore out that opinion and learned the hard way that stumbling around in the dark calls for prudence and sobriety rather than machismo and beer. It took a while, but my youthful motto of Catch Fish or Die Trying gradually matured into, as my guide friend Mark Bachmann says, Fish Long and Prosper. My reasons for going night fishing also evolved from recklessness to competitiveness to romance and finally to the pure journalistic impulse to just see what's going on when no one else is looking.

There were only eight fishermen in four canoes with miles of river to spread out in, and that may have accounted for the relaxed atmosphere at the put-in. (More than anything, we must have resembled a small group of men killing a few minutes before clocking in for the night shift.) Granted, the hatch was known to be winding down, but I'm told that even at its height it doesn't draw what you could call big crowds, even though anyone who cares anything about fishing knows about it.

A few days earlier, at a convenience store in the town of Hayward, a pierced, orange-haired girl spotted me for a fisherman (it must have been the hat), and we got to talking. She told me the Hex hatch was fading, but it was still sputtering off here and there on nights when it didn't rain. She also said she'd gotten a nice limit of big bluegills the previous afternoon at a secret spot, adding that it would have been more fun on a fly rod, but she'd promised a mess of fish for supper, so she played it safe and used a spinning rod and meal worms.

"Far out," I said, dating myself to the 1960s.

In the last few minutes before we launched from the bridge, there was the briefest and courtliest conversation about where we were all going. There was no jockeying for position, just a comparison of notes so no one would get in anyone else's way. Everyone seemed to have a certain bend in the river in mind, but no one was adamant. In that flat, swampy landscape, the river is nothing *but* big, lazy bends, and it's possible that on any given night one could be as good as another.

Once you're at your spot, you string up a rod and, while you can still see, tie on a big Hex dun. You leave the spent-wing flies in the box for now. If there's a spinner fall—which could turn out to be the main event—it will happen much later, say, around two a.m.

Then you slather yourself liberally with DEET because the mosquitoes are hellish and they're at their worst right at dusk. (Jim said the mosquitoes go away shortly after dark and I hoped he was right.) You also look behind you and try to memorize the location of anything that could snag your back cast. You know you'll lose your bearings later, but you go through the motions anyway.

Then you wait. Full darkness comes on gradually enough that your eyes adjust to it. You're wearing a headlamp, but the trick is not to use it because it will scare the fish and also ruin your night vision. You're not exactly standing at attention, but you don't take a load off by sitting on the bank, either. It's now maybe eleven o'clock at night; you're just getting started for the second time today and should be tired, but you're not. Half an hour later, you see a flashlight winking through the trees across the river and think it must be another night fisher hiking in. Then you see another and another and realize that they're not far away, but up close, and that they're lightning bugs.

The whining of mosquitoes still seemed deafening, but when the first trout rose, I could hear it clearly, although it was less clear exactly where it was. It may not be too simplistic to say that the pertinent fact about night fishing is that you can't see much.

It was cloudy with no moon or stars, but there was still enough vague, diffuse night shine that if I could get the angle just right I could make out odd patches of dull pewter that had to be the river, complete with scattered spots I took to be Hex duns and now and then the spreading rings of a rise. I'd done enough night fishing to know that you should look slightly to the side of whatever you want to see because your peripheral vision is more acute in the dark, but I had to remind myself to do that because I hadn't done enough for the sidelong glance to be second nature.

At one point, a big dun blundered into the side of my neck, and although I'm not normally creeped out by bugs and had expected something like that, I still swiped it away a little too quickly. When I felt the tickle of another fly landing on the back of my hand, I caught him in a cage made of a loose fist. I could feel him in there and he felt huge, but he was also nearly weightless, and it was disorienting to have the same sense telling me he was there and also that he wasn't.

I was casting in the dark and setting the hook by sound and hunch, so there's no telling how many strikes I missed, but I know I nicked and lost three or four trout and landed two. I'll say one was fourteen inches long and the other more like sixteen, but then I don't guess fish size very accurately even when I can see them. Now and then, I'd hear quiet splashing from where Jim, Ken, and Bob were spread out downstream, but nothing that sounded like an anvil being dropped in the water and no yelling, so I guessed they were doing about the same. The mythology of night fishing always leaves one thing out: It *is* true that the biggest trout often feed at night and that some of the real monsters are entirely nocturnal, but normal-sized trout feed at night, too, and they're the ones you're most likely to catch.

The hatch petered out about the time a foggy, misting rain started, and not long after that I saw a headlamp bobbing toward me. It was Jim coming to say the hatch was over and the rain would cancel any spinner fall there might have been, so we might as well head back. "We'll try again tomorrow night after you guys get in from bass fishing," he added.

I hesitated a single beat at the prospect of back-to-back twenty-hour days of fishing. (I sometimes have to remind myself that I'm no longer a twenty-four-year-old manual laborer with the stamina of a Farmall tractor.) Then I said, "You bet."

On the trip back upstream to the bridge, I was paddling from the bow and helpfully turned on my headlamp, but Jim asked me to shut it off. "Just paddle," he said, "I'll steer." The mistake I'd made was to temporarily blind us both, and when I turned off the light and was greeted by absolute darkness, I had a disjointed memory of a gag painting I'd once seen somewhere. It was a totally black canvas titled *Night Fishing*.

5

THE PERFECT HOST

There are similarities between being an actual guide and just taking someone fishing, but the big difference is that when it's informal, no money changes hands. Most guided trips work out because guides have inherently generous natures (except those who have done it for too long and are nearing burnout), while most clients understand that fishing is so unpredictable that the only thing the guide really controls is what's for lunch. Still, the blunt fact that one person is paying and the other is being paid can take on a peculiar and not altogether pleasant life of its own. In the best circumstances, that's all but unnoticeable, but at other times it becomes the central characteristic of the relationship. Most of us, given the choice, would rather be a helpful friend than an employee.

I took two people fishing recently: my old friend Ed Engle and Tomonori Higashi (a.k.a. "Billy") a fisherman, writer, and translator from Japan. This could have looked like a business trip, since Billy had translated Ed's book on bamboo fly rod makers, *Splitting Cane,* into Japanese and was about to begin translating one of mine. But the truth is, we just fished together for a few days, and business never came up except for a discussion of the niceties of translation in general, most of which I had to take on faith because I never learned a second language. For instance, Billy said he'd had to change the title of Ed's book because *Splitting Cane* came out literally in Japanese as something like *Tearing Grass* and made no sense.

We started fishing on a drainage an hour's drive north of home, up a tributary creek in the neighborhood of 9,000 feet. I've always liked this stream because it flows out of a long, narrow, roadless canyon, it's tipped at a steep angle that produces lots of luscious pocket water, it holds more fish than the larger river it feeds into, and it's spectacularly beautiful. There's not much more you can reasonably ask of a trout stream.

The fishing was good to the usual high country mixed bag of browns, brook trout, rainbows, and cutthroats, plus Ed's single rainbow-cutthroat hybrid. We hiked in pretty far, scrambling over boulders and deadfall along the stream and then climbing back up to the narrow trail when it was time to move to another stretch. Billy kept right up, but during a break late in the afternoon he finally admitted he was "feeling the altitude," and I was embarrassed for not thinking of that. Thirty-six hours earlier, he'd been near sea level in Yokohama, and here he was climbing around in the thin air at 9,000 feet, sleep-deprived and jet-lagged. Oddly enough, it was right about then that the water began to rise and get muddy from an unseen thunder-storm upstream, so we could quit without Billy feeling that he'd dragged us away from the fishing.

The next day, we four-wheeled up a dirt road along another high-altitude stream (so there'd be less hiking) and did well again on the same mix of fish. This was a little creek that usually fishes well at that time of year but that also has a moody streak, so I was glad it showed off well with sparse hatches of mayflies, caddis, and some small stoneflies. There wasn't the pressure of real guiding, as I mentioned, but you still want to be a good host who at least knows where and when to fish in his own back yard.

Billy turned out to be a skilled and astute fisherman. He said the small streams here reminded him of those in Japan except that ours were wilder, prettier, and had bigger trout. (That may or may not have been strictly true, but it was a nice thing to say.) He took a few photos, and several times I spotted him just standing quietly, looking around and taking it all in, which I take as the sign of a true connoisseur. He wanted to know the names of some birds, which I was able to tell him, and he was fascinated and a little worried when Ed gathered some boletus mushrooms that we planned to eat with dinner. I told him I trusted Ed's wild-mushroom identifications with my life (literally) but that neither of us would be insulted if he didn't eat any. He did try a few that night and said they were good.

Billy also got along well with Meatball, my rescued alley cat—who is not a classically likable kitty—and was delighted by the mother raccoon with six young kits that had been visiting my back porch most evenings for reasons of their own. In fact, if there was anything about the fishing or the accommodations that disappointed him, you'd never have known it, but then he *does* come from a culture that values politeness above almost everything else. Of course, we Americans value politeness, too, it's just that we don't practice it rigorously.

Not long after Ed and Billy headed off to try some big trout water on the West Slope, my friend Jim Babb came out to fish for a week. Jim now lives in Maine, but he arrived there by an elaborately circuitous route that began in East Tennessee, where he grew up fishing the small trout streams in the Smoky Mountains. (You'll hear his travels in his accent, which can have echoes of the southern mountains and Down East Maine in the same sentence.)

By now Jim has fished around much of the world, but has never lost his sentimental attachment to the kinds of small water he grew up fishing, so although there are decidedly snazzier places to fish in Colorado, he specifically wanted to see the small, high-altitude trout creeks that are my home water.

You automatically compare new water to what you're familiar with as a way of guessing how much of what you already know might apply. After the first day, Jim said that aside from obvious differences like elevation and the surrounding vegetation, these little creeks in the northern Colorado Rockies might as well be in the Smokies back home. (I could have guessed that by the casual, efficient way he fished them.) We agreed that there's something irresistible about out-of-the-way creeks like this that are saved from the depredations of fly-fishing tourism by being what many would call undistinguished.

The daily program was to four-wheel in to a stretch of stream remote enough that we were unlikely to meet another fisherman and leapfrog up it using a neat system Jim had taught me on a previous trip to Colorado: When you start fishing, the first thing you do is build a three-rock cairn in some obvious place—like a midstream bounder—so the guy coming along behind you knows where you started. When you come on one of these, you kick it over to avoid confusion at some later date, hike upstream above your partner to fresh, unfished water and build your own temporary landmark as a signal to *him*.

In fact, it was this system that tipped me off that I'd lost Jim one day. I'd passed him and had given him plenty of leeway before getting back into the stream, erecting my little rock pile and starting to fish again. The trout were biting well that day and I was engrossed, so it was quite a while later that I realized I hadn't come to a cairn and hadn't seen Jim pass me. He's not the type either to pound any one spot for long or to rush far ahead thinking there's something better upstream. In other words, his fishing pace was entirely familiar, and it was clear that I'd somehow gotten way out in front of him.

I reeled in, got out of the water, and hiked back downstream to look for him. I was just curious at first, but when I walked all the way down to my last cairn and found that it was still there, I started to worry. It was probably an hour and a half since I'd piled up those three flat rocks, and at the time, Jim couldn't have been more than fifteen minutes behind me.

I hiked downstream to where I'd last seem him and then made my way up to the logging road we'd come in on and walked back to the truck, since that's always the default position when there's either trouble or confusion. That's where I found him.

It turned out that right after I'd passed him the last time, he'd used a downed spruce log as a step going down a steep bank, but it was rotten. It gave way under his weight and dumped him several feet into the creek, where he landed thigh-first on a pyramid-shaped rock. The leg wasn't broken, but it hurt as much as if it were (he learned later that the bone was bruised) so he had slowly and painfully hobbled back to the truck. As an afterthought, he said he'd managed not to break the irreplaceable fifty-year-old F. E. Thomas bamboo rod I'd lent him. Believe it or not, I hadn't even thought about that.

The short version of the story is, Jim turned down a visit to the doctor, accepted some ibuprofen, and insisted on fishing the next day, even though it hurt like hell to put weight on the leg. For that matter, it was painful enough just to watch, but I understood what he was up to. If you get a little sick or slightly injured on a fishing trip, but you're not actually debilitated, you simply suck it up and keep fishing, usually more out of stubbornness than actual bravery. From my own experience, I can say that a bad back makes you hike slower, stove-up knees keep you from wading confidently, tendonitis of the elbow buggers your casting, and a dose of giardia can send you dashing into the bushes fifteen times in an afternoon, but although none of this is fun, it's discernibly better than not fishing.

The only change in plans was that I bagged the big finale I was quietly saving for the last day. It was a lovely little willow-choked, high-altitude cutthroat stream, but the sweet spot is at the end of a long, grueling uphill hike and I didn't think Jim could make it in his present condition. Maybe I should have discussed this with him and let him decide for himself. After all, he was limping badly and wincing now and then, but otherwise getting around okay and catching the hell out of fish. But in the end, I never even mentioned the stream's existence. It was an executive decision for which I take full responsibility.

I'd pictured Jim going home at the end of the week where he could rest and recuperate, but it turned out he *wasn't* going home; he was flying out to Oregon to fish with a mutual friend for a while. It did seem to make a kind of sense: Why cancel the next leg of a perfectly good fishing trip just because you can barely walk?

A day or so after I dropped Jim off at the airport, my neighbor, Dana, came over and asked me if I'd teach him how to fly-fish.

"Oh, sure," I said, "No problem."

The fact is, I owed the guy at least that small favor and couldn't possibly say no, so why bother telling him I suck as a guide and casting instructor? If I botched the lesson and he didn't give up the sport out of disgust, he could always hire someone who knew what he was doing.

Luckily, Dana turned out to be a natural. He immediately grasped the principle that you're casting the *line* and the fly just trails along, and also that the rod is a long flexible lever that does most of the work for you, so you don't have to work as hard as most beginners do. Beyond that, he watched, and understood and followed directions, which is all it takes. It probably didn't hurt that he has studied martial arts for years and is a harpsichord maker by trade, so he was fully capable of both athleticism and delicacy. By the end of the lesson, he was double-hauling sixty feet of line.

After a week of practice (he actually practiced!), it was time to go fishing. By way of formulating a strategy, I thought of some of the great, wise, patient guides I'd fished with—as well as some of the dimmer bulbs—but when we got to the stream, I still didn't have much of a plan. The time to be generous had arrived and I could only hope it would come naturally.

There was that first awkward moment when it becomes obvious that casting on a stream is not like casting on a lawn, if only because the lawn isn't moving, but after a few tries Dana took to it easily. He caught his first trout ever on a fly rod (a ten-inch brown), then his second, and so on. I thought, This must be what it's like to have a star pupil, although that warm glow usually comes after considerably more effort from the teacher.

On the drive home, Dana asked about tackle, and I tried to explain how complicated the sport can get if you let it. He said he wasn't worried; that he only wanted to fish the local creeks and figured a rod and reel, a few flies, and some other odds and ends would get him by.

I told him he was absolutely right—that with just a little attentiveness, this one little corner of life could be kept simple. I didn't say that *I'd* kept it simple; just that I knew it could be done.

6

BAJA

Ed and I have just checked into the Hotel Punta Colorada near the southern tip of Baja in Mexico. (Nearly everything on the coast is named for either a *punta* or a *cabo*—a point or a cape.) After we rode for an hour and a half from the airport in an old but air-conditioned van, the desert heat hit us like an anvil, so we're sitting in the small stone courtyard, barefoot in the shade, trying to acclimate. There's a slight breeze blowing inland from the Sea of Cortez. It's hot and humid, but it *is* a breeze.

We're supposed to meet Mike Rieser, our friend, guide, and half owner of the Baja Flyfishing Company, but it's early enough that he's still out on the water with clients. In fact, everyone is probably still out on the water, which would explain why the place is nearly deserted. There's only one person in sight: a young, broad-shouldered guy standing across the courtyard looking at a garish banner announcing the 41ST ANNUAL ROOST-ERFISH TOURNAMENT that we won't be taking part in. The back of his T-shirt says, SECOND PLACE IS JUST THE FIRST LOSER.

I abandoned some of my vices years ago for the usual reasons, but a sudden blast from the past informs me that a cold beer and a joint would really hit the spot right now. We're less than a day out of Denver by jet and car, but already such thoughts come naturally, possibly because we Americans have such a long history of using this country as an excuse for bad behavior. Decades before Las Vegas coined its now-famous slogan (What Happens in Vegas *Stays* in Vegas) I met some bass fishers in Texas who had agreed among themselves that whatever happened in Mexico never happened.

When it comes to fishing trips to strange new places, Ed has what he calls the "three-day rule." You naturally fish from your first tentative cast as if it mattered (because it does) and you might even catch some fish, but the first day is nonetheless spent trying to gain some sense of where you are. This process actually continues through the trip and lingers a while even after you're home, but the foreignness is most vivid at the beginning when even the birdcalls are just pretty gibberish. You'll hear about travelers who are so experienced that they "feel at home anywhere," but I always thought the idea was to go far enough to feel a little lost.

By the end of the second day, you've begun to absorb the daily routine of fishing—which is slightly different everywhere—and the most common elements of your surroundings are no longer a constant surprise. The ubiquitous brown, chattery birds turn out to be cactus wrens, and the bright yellow and black birds nesting in the palm trees are yellow-backed orioles. The small desert iguanas are said not to taste like chicken at all, but pretty much like iguana. There's also the sound, smell, and colors of the sea, the brown pelicans and frigatebirds and the burden of my personal language barrier. I'd never been to Mexico before except for a quick trip to a border town in the 1960s, the memory of which is now mercifully vague, so my pigeon Spanish only extends to phrases like, *"Dónde está el baño, por favor?"* (Where is the toilet, please?) And, *"Hola, señor*, do you speak *Ingles?"*

It's possible to feel like an idiot trying to communicate by pointing and grunting, and an actual conversation is unthinkable, but then I often get tired of listening to people gab, and when you can't understand what they're saying, the effect can be akin to silence.

By the third day—either on your own or with coaching—you've picked up a smattering of fishing techniques, like the "scissor strip," where you sweep the rod with one hand while stripping line with the other to give your streamer a realistic final burst of speed. You're retrieving like mad anyway when a roosterfish comes for the fly, but without that panicked acceleration from his prey, he's likely to smell a rat and lose interest at the last crucial second.

This third day is when a kind of working familiarity kicks in and things begin to fall into place: not everything by a long shot, but sometimes enough to make a difference. It seems like luck—and in a way it is—but it's the kind you can court by paying attention.

That initial sense of strangeness is still there, but it's receded to the point that you're no longer walking around with your mouth hanging open. Still, it's best not to start getting careless. For instance, that was the day a passing peddler said to me, "Eh, *señor*," and flashed a battered valise filled with jewelry. I liked his friendly, conspiratorial grin and bought a silver and turquoise bracelet for my lady back home at a price that made me think it was stolen. Later, I was told you're *supposed* to think it's stolen so you'll enjoy the implied larceny of the transaction. In fact, the bracelet was cheap because it was fake (the turquoise was blue plastic), but to be fair, the guy never said it wasn't. And anyway, it's the thought that counts, right?

The roosterfish that were our main quarry on this trip seemed oddly ornamental. Picture an elongated bluegill-shaped fish with a deeply forked tail and a dorsal fin consisting of seven long, thin rays that stick up like the tines of a pitchfork to more than the height of the body. The overall color is an iridescent bluish, greenish, silvery white with a dark back and two wide black racing stripes that start under the dorsal fin and sweep sinuously back to the tail. Most of our roosters were in the eight to ten pound class, but they get much bigger. Mike said he's seen some sixty pounders. As with all fish, even a good photo doesn't quite do them justice.

Mike thinks roosterfish use those dorsal rays to either herd or disorient baitfish because in the last split second before they strike at a trolled bait or a retrieved streamer they'll flash up beside it, wave that fin, and then strike to the side with something like a sucker punch. This happens so fast that it leaves only the fleeting impression of spikes in the water, but if you've fished in the region for thirty years as Mike has, you'll have gotten used to the way things happen with such blinding suddenness.

Fishing here is anything but a contemplative sport, especially when you're on the beach chasing roosterfish. In order to cover the number of miles it can take to locate fish, you drive an all-terrain vehicle, sometimes slowly; other times at speeds you later think might not have been prudent. You have hot desert on one side, cool surf on the other, and nothing much in front except sand, driftwood, and the occasional spavined free-range steer. You're carrying two rods: a 10-weight rigged with a size 4 Clouser Minnow for smaller fish and a 12-weight with a big fly for the *grandes*.

If you're fishing with Mike, your large fly will probably be a Gym Sock, an aptly named mullet pattern that catches fish but that casts like a piece of dirty laundry. The borrowed 12-weight rod itself is designed as a compromise between casting a fly line and playing a big fish. It's an imperfect bargain between too much rod and not enough. You'd get used to it eventually, but it would take more time than you have.

The idea is to spot fish busting up bait near shore or herding small fish into the wave trough right at the surf line where they're effectively cornered. You'll know the guy on the ATV in front of you has spotted a big cruiser when he pours on the speed to get ahead of it or does a skidding U-turn and shoots back past you with a fiendish look in his eyes.

You're barefoot because any kind of footwear will immediately fill with fine sand and abrade your feet like emery cloth.

When you first hop off the ATV, the hot sand burns your feet and you run for the water as much to cool your soles as to chase fish. You're in a big hurry, but you're careful not to step on a jaggedly broken shell, a crab, or the spiny body of a dead puffer fish. Once you are there, the surf can seem as if it wants to knock you down and drag you out to sea, and the water can be filled with chunks of dead jellyfish that have been churned into pieces by the waves. They sting your feet and bare legs painfully, but they're harmless unless you get a big piece. You learn not to complain because the only known remedy is urine—your own or someone else's.

Once a fish is spotted and you're on foot, you can end up covering hundreds of yards of beach at a dead run—high-stepping in the surf and false casting as you go—before you hook the fish, he finally pulls ahead of you, or you just give up. Then you reel in and trudge back to your ATV, which by then is a hot red dot on the horizon. The weariness and dehydration don't hit until you're back outside your room sitting in the only available shade for miles around, swearing that if you do this again you'll train for it first. A few weeks of jogging in Death Valley would do it.

Fishing from a *panga* was slightly less frantic, and since the craft was only twenty-three feet from bow to stern, there was no running. Mostly, it was just the amiable boredom of grown men out in a boat, punctuated by the usual moments of sheer panic.

They said it was cool for June, but it was still hot by any reasonable standard, although the humidity depended on whether the prevailing wind was blowing out of the east across the Sea of Cortez or from the west across the desert. Some days were anywhere from bearable to almost comfortable. Other days you'd fry like bacon.

Sometimes we'd come on a pod of ladyfish busting up a bait ball: a school of thousands of sardines huddled together in a single amorphous mass in the vain hope of safety in numbers. The charcoal gray bait ball would be moving and billowing slowly, and as the ladyfish sliced through it, their mirrored sides would flash in the sun. Mike said the sight reminded him of lightning in a storm cloud. Now and then something larger but unseen would attack the ball, and it would break into two pieces for a second before coalescing in the monster's wake.

Ladyfish are a kind of small tarpon, and what they're doing is blasting through the school a few times, killing, maiming, and dismembering a dozen sardines at every pass. Then they'll drop down below the school and pick off the dead and dying as they sink toward the bottom. As tempting as it was to cast and strip fast, Mike said no, just let the weighted streamer sink and hope a fish mistakes it for a casualty. My overall impression of the little bit of saltwater fishing I've done is of just this kind of speed and violence. As I'd let my streamer sink through a count of twenty seconds, I'd have time to think, This is a hell of a long way from trout sipping mayflies.

Another common fishing method is called bait and switch, where a live baitfish is trolled behind the boat to attract game fish that the fishermen then cast to. Naturally, there's a science to this. You usually use sardines, but if you're hoping for something bigger, you try a larger mullet. The bait has to be trolled within the clients' casting range (this would be closer for some than for others), and of course when the fish come, the bait has to be kept away from them so that, with any luck, they'll go for the flies.

The fish come suddenly and unexpectedly, usually in the

middle of a lazy conversation about the old days, and they're sometimes there and gone so quickly you'll have only one quick shot. It's impossible to stay tightly wound for hours on end, so you try for a kind of subconscious hair trigger while trying not to be standing on your line.

Mike's partner John Matson told me he sometimes gets clients who have never seen or heard of this and who are reticent about fly fishing over chum. He said the cure is to take them out on featureless blue water without a fish in sight and ask, "Okay, where do you want to cast?"

So the first order of business after you've met your captain at the dock in the morning is to motor south along the coast looking for men drifting in small boats selling bait. They're called *sardinieros* after the sardines they catch in throw nets, although some will have mullet instead or, amazingly, eight-to-ten-inch bonefish. Their bait wells are the boats themselves, dangerously half filled with seawater. These guys don't motor to a predetermined location but just drift wherever they happen to be. It's up to the *gringo* sports in the big fancy boats to come and find them.

You might see these same guys later the same day, fishing with hand lines from *pangas* or from shore for fish that they'll either eat or sell to a buyer up the coast in La Ribera. In fact, you haven't done this properly until you've motored past a couple of these men catching dorado literally hand over fist with hand lines wound on sticks of driftwood while you stand there fishless holding a thousand dollars worth of fly rod and reel. They nod cordially as you motor past, though not without a touch of condescension. There's the temptation to envy such a simple, uncluttered existence, although in your heart you know that hard day-to-day subsistence with no safety net would suck.

Once the bait was in the well, Mike would examine it and discuss it with the captain in his fluent Spanish. The size and condition of the fish and where they were netted could provide valuable information on currents, water temperatures, and the possible location of game fish. Mike's favorite captain was a man named Tico, a dignified gray-haired gentleman of indeterminate age who was said to speak some English but preferred not to. He was quiet and could seem stern and aloof, but then when someone hooked a roosterfish, he might smile to himself and make quiet chicken noises.

True to Ed's three-day rule, it was on the afternoon of the third day that I hooked something big. We were trolling large streamers on 12-weights, and when the fish struck, we didn't know what it was, although I'm glad Mike had reminded me to hold on tight to the rod. As it turned out, it would be a while before we saw the fish, but Mike quickly deduced from the way it was fighting that it was a jack crevalle and then, sometime later, that it was a pretty big one.

I'll try to keep this short. When we finally got it in the boat, it ended up weighing just short of forty pounds, which Mike said is about as big as this species gets in those waters. It was the first one of these things I'd ever caught and an egregious example of unearned beginner's luck.

An experienced saltwater fisherman could have landed it more quickly, but it took me the better part of an hour and forty-five minutes, during which I poured sweat and my arms and shoulders burned and twitched involuntarily. Battling a big fish this long is supposed to be an epic business, but except for the excitement, it felt like single-handedly unloading a truck full of sod in hundred-degree heat. It occurred to me that a sane man might wonder why this is considered fun.

After a little too much time spent staring into the waves while standing on a pitching deck, the possibility of blowing lunch arose, but I found that all I had to do was look west, locate the blessedly stationary peaks of the Sierra de la Giganta in the distance and everything would be temporarily okay.

An hour into the fight, Mike leaned over and looked into my eyes.

"What!" I said.

"Just wanted to see if you were about to pass out," he answered. I guess that happens from time to time. They call it heatstroke, which sounds more manly than fainting.

I didn't see the fish until well into the fight, when I spotted him side-on in a ten-foot roller a little higher than my head. This was just before he sounded and had to be laboriously pumped back up. Out in the air, he'd be an almost disappointing dull aluminum color, but in the water he was all shades of electric blue-green and silver and didn't seem entirely real. He looked impossibly huge, but also nowhere near big enough to put up that kind of fight on that kind of tackle, but then there's a reason why the locals call these things *toros*.

Ed was shooting photo after photo, "trying to get the grimace just right," he said later, and also because, for the better part of two hours, there was nothing else to do.

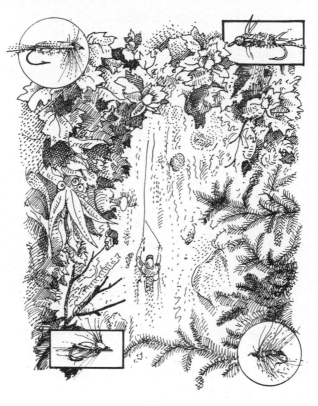

7

TENNESSEE

We were in the Unicoi Mountains in East Tennessee: a neighboring range of the Smoky Mountains, which are in turn part of the Appalachians that stretch from northern Georgia through northern Maine and roughly comprise the native range of brook trout in what is now the United States. (The first step is always to locate yourself physically, even if it's only the abbreviated, guidebook version.)

More specifically, we were fishing for trout in some of the

branches of the Tellico River at elevations of 2,000 to 3,000 feet in dense mixed forests of tulip poplar, hemlock, white pine, beech, oak, gum, maple, rhododendron, mountain laurel, flame azalea, and so on. These are verdant, ancient, round-shouldered mountains thousands of feet lower than the Rockies and ten times older, with forests that are a riot of species diversity and the humid climate that makes them prone to the morning mist that gave the Smokies their name.

I've lived virtually all of my adult life in Colorado, where snowcapped 14,000-foot peaks are a normal feature of the horizon, and have developed the predictable brand of chauvinism about this high, craggy country that induces altitude sickness in flatlanders. But as we drove into the Unicois, I was careful not to make the same faux pas I'd once committed in Pennsylvania, where I'd asked my host if we were getting close to the Appalachian Mountains. He said, "We're *in* 'em," and without thinking I said, "What, these little bumps?"

I faltered only once when we pulled off a paved road at the highest point in the Unicois: a whopping 4,000-some feet above sea level. As we admired the view—which was actually pretty impressive—I couldn't help pointing out that if we were standing in front of my house in Colorado, we'd be 2,000 feet underground, and I'm only in the foothills.

At first glance from a car window—and later on foot—these mountains seemed inviting but impenetrable. It was spring, with comfortable days and cool nights, and the mountain laurel bushes were coming into bloom. They were beautiful, with the flowers shading from white at lower altitudes to pale pink to rose as you gained elevation. But there are places called "laurel hells" where these large shrubs are so thick and intertwined that you couldn't go ten feet through them without crawling on your belly. There are similar rhododendron hells as well as a bush known as dog hobble because not even hunting dogs can get through it. Which is to say, off-trail hiking is best left to those who know the country.

This is the kind of aggressively lush habitat that can swallow unused trails, dirt roads, and even whole farmsteads in a matter of a few seasons. I was impressed by this country's ability to erase minor human sign so quickly and caught myself wishing my own home region was that resilient. In southern Wyoming, not that far over the border from where I live, there are places where the sage and rabbitbush haven't yet reclaimed the wheel ruts left by the Overland Stage Route that was abandoned in the late 1860s.

Besides the impregnable vegetation, local hazards can include aggressive white-faced hornets, copperheads, and timber rattlers (black snakes are evil-looking but harmless), the occasional troublesome black bear and "Russian hogs"—wild boars once imported from Europe for rich sportsmen to hunt, now long since gone wild and hunted by those who are anything *but* rich.

If you weren't raised on a farm, your nightmares probably don't include pigs, but the first time you come on a place where, in the normal course of rooting for food, a two-hundred-pound boar has Rototilled a quarter acre with its tusks, uprooting fifteen-foot saplings in the process, the potential for trouble begins to take shape. On the other hand, the local cuisine depends largely on pork, and word is, these wild hogs taste the way God intended for pigs to taste.

Spiders are usually more of a nuisance than a threat, but they're everywhere in great numbers, and when someone says to "get you a spider pole," he doesn't mean a kind of fishing rod, as I first thought, but a handy stick to wipe away the webs as you pick your way through the woods or wade up a stream. Of course, spider webs across a narrow creek are a sure sign that no one else has fished there recently, so you're happy to see them.

All that makes the place sound prickly and dangerous, but of course it's not. It's just that in any new country there are a few things you should know, if only so you don't learn them the hard way. Also, it's not unheard of for locals to practice a little harmless exaggeration on visitors, possibly as payback for the implied wisecrack about their little mountains.

This was a fishing trip, but it was also sort of a left-handed family reunion, since I was fishing with my distant cousin Jim Babb and his brother Walter. Ever since Jim and I discovered it by accident while we were stranded together in a cabin in Labrador, the family connection has seemed tenuous to me (a Babb cousin was once married to a cousin of my mother's). But there's something hospitable about this southern mountain culture that's eager to assume you're kin until proven otherwise and a far-removed cousin is greeted like a lost brother. Genealogy is a kind of folk art here, and it's possible to follow faint bloodlines far enough that you end up related to either Davy Crockett or Dolly Parton. I've witnessed a similar phenomenon in Texas, where every native can trace his ancestry back to the Alamo, although not always to the same side of the wall.

I'd known Jim for a number of years, and when I first met Walter at his home in Sweetwater, I was struck by the similarities between the two brothers. Walter is two years older and Jim defers to him in matters of local fishing, but otherwise they seem like two versions of the same man, one who left home and one who didn't.

Walter is one of those fishermen you used to meet often but who are now becoming a threatened species in our mobile culture. He started fishing the Tellico River drainage at age six or seven when he was barely old enough to hold a fly rod. He liked it there, so he stayed, and now, at age sixty, he has fished the same water continually for over half a century using the same flies and the same upstream wet-fly cast he and Jim learned from their father. He's retired now—in the modern sense that he still works, but at a different job—and makes a living tying flies and building lovely bamboo fly rods that sell for less than most only because he's largely unknown outside the region. He also guided for a while but has since given it up. He said he had to fish with too many people he wouldn't have gone with if he weren't being paid and the pay wasn't enough to make up for the aggravation. When I asked him what his ambitions were as a rod maker, he said that if he could sell a dozen rods a year he could pay for his health insurance.

When you're in a new place you like for a short time, it's possible to come away feeling at a loss. You'll learn a few place names and remember that a slingshot is called a "stone whip," but genuine knowledge of a region goes bone-deep and stretches back through generations. This time though, I picked up more than the usual smattering of the natural and cultural history by asking occasional questions, but mostly just by listening to a week's worth of reminiscences between the brothers. This amounted to a stream-of-consciousness documentary full of low-rent shenanigans and populated by people with names like Creepy, Pea Head, Paddle Foot, and Tater Chip. (The trick to reading southern writers is simply to understand that they're not kidding.)

Small streams, spooky trout that seldom rise to dry flies, difficult to nearly impossible casting conditions, and a kind of hard-edged local practicality dictate the region's peculiar wet-fly fishing style. It was first developed for the native Appalachian brook trout but now works every bit as well on the introduced rainbows and browns.

You fish a brace of flies: a fairly large weighted nymph (usually something resembling a golden stonefly) with a smaller unweighted wet fly off the leader above it on a short dropper. The Babb brothers both favored a Blackburn Tellico with a Speck on the dropper, but other patterns also worked. These are small streams, and the runs and pockets you're fishing are usually shallow, so there's no added weight beyond the heavy nymph, partly because you don't need it and partly because lead on a leader deadens the subtle take and makes it harder to detect. Local fishermen often carry three versions of the same stonefly nymph in three different weights for different depths of water and current speeds, color-coded by the thread color on the head.

I won't try to describe the cast and drift in detail because I'm not sure I can. It's a little like wet fly fishing only backward, with an upstream instead of a downstream cast. Or maybe it's like short-line nymphing, only with a longer line and no strike indicator, or a case of parallel evolution with Czech nymphing in the same way that octopus and human eyes are surprisingly similar, but still not identical or interchangeable. Differences in regional fishing techniques are sometimes so subtle as to be all but imperceptible, but they also tend to be real and effective. If you're like me, you'll think, Yeah, that's nothing new, and then have to be told and shown and then told and shown again when you don't quite get it. Of course, instruction is helpful and so is watching someone who's good at it, but nothing measures up to half a century of constant practice. In the end, it's the trout that will tell you when you've got it right.

One thing I *can* pass on is the necessity of striking parallel to the water instead of upward. In most places, the forest canopy is so low that if you strike up on a missed take, you'll put your flies far out of reach in the branches above. If you strike sideways and miss, your flies will still be tangled up, but they'll often be low enough to reach.

Some of my own flies from home worked, but the local patterns worked better, which is as it should be. The traditional fly patterns of the region arose in relative isolation from the mainstream of eastern fly fishing and without easy access to the usual exotic feathers, so they were tied mostly with the materials at hand: little-known patterns like the Speck, George Nymph, Crow Fly, Rattler, and the Yellerhammer, a palmer-style fly that was first tied from the split primary feathers of a common woodpecker known to most as a yellow-shafted flicker. Modern commercial Yellerhammers are tied with substitute dyed hackles, but a man known for tying the original versions with flicker feathers was once heard to tell a game warden, "I know it's illegal to shoot 'em, but the damned things keep dyin' of natural causes in my yard."

We stayed in Walter's cabin, which was far enough up the slope from the Tellico River that we couldn't see the water, but not so far that we couldn't hear it on quiet nights. This is a simple frame cabin with one side propped on flimsy-looking stilts to accommodate the steep slope, and it's painted one of those colors that don't exactly grab your attention. I remember it as some shade of green, but it could just as easily have been gray or blue. The place has everything a fisherman needs and not much else. (The womenfolk do come here from time to time, but not often enough to exert their domestic influence.) The only interior decoration is a collection of fish mounts from what Walter calls his "taxidermy period": locally caught rainbow and brown trout of surprising size for such small water.

We did fish the Tellico one day, mostly to collect the main ingredient for a dinner of trout fried in bacon grease, fried potatoes and onions with bacon, and green beans cooked with salt pork. Another night we had a side dish of poke, a peppery wild vegetable that Walter gathered beside a dirt road. This was also cooked in pork fat. You believe you can eat like this as long as you hike and wade miles a day, although I'm told the condition of your arteries isn't always reflected by your waistline.

The Tellico is a pretty, medium-sized trout river that's stocked every week using what seems to be a reasonable and efficient system for a put-and-take fishery: It's closed to fishing for two days a week while it's being stocked (to let the fish spread out a little and to keep eager fishermen from chasing the stocking trucks). Then the stream opens for the next five days, including the weekend, when it gets crowded if not exactly mobbed. You have to buy a daily permit to fish the river, and the proceeds from that go directly back into the well-funded stocking program, making the whole thing function as a kind of perpetual motion machine.

This struck me as a sweet deal. A stocked fishery is a shadow of the real thing, but it can fulfill a need and, in this case, it takes nearly all the pressure off the small feeder creeks where the trout are wild. The permit costs less than a trout dinner in any restaurant, the dinner itself—cooked by Jim and Walter (I did the dishes)—was better than most, and the ambience of the kitchen table was unbeatable.

That one grocery run aside, we spent the rest of our days fishing the smaller branches far from the main river. One of these (a pretty good one) was located right along a county road, but most of the rest involved several miles of driving on dirt roads and then several more miles on foot to reach. These streams each had their own character, but were also similar: small, mossy, and slippery, with dense, low canopies that kept the water in perpetual shade but also grabbed your back cast. Sometimes there were impressive waterfalls that became less lovely when you realized you'd have to climb past them to keep fishing. The trout were mostly bright, strong rainbows with the odd brown thrown in, and if you got high enough up a drainage, you could begin to pick up remnant brook trout.

We'd always start up a trail at a fairly brisk pace and within minutes Walter would have pulled far ahead and gone out of sight. He wasn't racing us or trying to hurry us along; he's just one of those guys who has only one speed. Half a mile up the trail, we'd find him waiting patiently. Jim said no one could keep up with Walter even when they were kids fishing with their father, so he'd set off by himself, covering vast amounts of real estate on his own and invariably coming back late, but with a limit of trout. Jim added that if their mother had known how far Walter was allowed to go into these mountains alone at such a tender age, she'd have had a fit, so to keep peace at home it was never mentioned.

We leapfrogged upstream using the method Jim had taught me back in Colorado, the one where you build a little cairn of rocks to mark your starting point so the fisherman coming behind you knows that the water upstream has already been fished. When I first tried this, my tendency was to build for monumental size to make sure the thing was noticed, but then I realized that even a simple three-rock cairn clashed with the intentions of nature to the extent that it stood out like a billboard, even among thousands of similar rocks placed by time, current, and gravity. It's sad to say, but almost everything we humans do in a natural environment amounts to a sore thumb.

Jim and Walter have been doing this since they were kids— long enough to have developed distinct personal styles. Walter's cairns were always the same: quick and dirty, consisting of any three randomly selected rocks that could be stacked without falling over. Jim's reflected his mood of the day and the materials at hand, ranging from a few quickly piled rocks to the full-blown prehistoric-style fertility goddess he left for me one day, complete with a small head, pregnant belly, and pendulous breasts. It must have taken half an hour to build—most of it spent finding the right rocks—and it seemed a shame to kick it over, but you have to in order not to confuse other fishermen or yourself on a different day. It may have been a borderline work of art, but like everything else man-made, its fate was to be temporary.

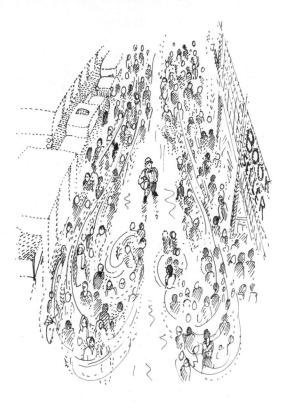

8

BOOK TOUR

On my most recent book tour, I was invited by some people at
a radio station in Oregon to float the Deschutes River. I travel
light on book tours, with just a carry-on and no fishing gear, so
I'd have had to fish with borrowed tackle while doing a recorded
interview to be broadcast later. It would have been a short day
because I had to get back early to make myself presentable and
get to a bookstore in time for a signing that evening.

I did give it some thought—one does not blithely turn down

a float on the Deschutes—but in the end I asked if we could just do the interview in the studio instead. On the face of it, this trip on the river might have sounded like a decent idea and potentially good radio, but the few times I've done similar things, they just haven't worked out.

There are several examples, but the most vivid mental picture that comes to mind is of a guide friend rowing away from a beautiful Blue-winged Olive hatch on the Bow River in Alberta because I had to be at a book signing in Calgary in an hour. I made it with minutes to spare and said, "I'm happy to be here" because that's just what you say.

There were some other attempts, but eventually trying to sneak in a few hours of fishing in the middle of what amounts to a business trip began to strike me as pointless. You're rushed and your mind is on other things, so the best you can do is go through the motions while worrying about what comes next, which is just no way to fish. Honestly, if I have time to kill, I'd rather wander around a strange city gawking at the big buildings while the crowd parts around me like current around a rock.

There was also a kind of built-in phoniness to the few staged interviews I've done on the water that I could never get past. You know, "Here we are on the river fishing with angling author John Gierach . . ." Well, yeah, technically, but what we're really doing is performing a media stunt in which you're expected to catch a fish not for its own sake, but for show, and once that realization has taken hold, I'm not a good enough actor to pretend it hasn't. The result is that I can end up giving the kind of sketchy interview that defeats the purpose.

Those are the arguments and I stand by them, but the real reason is selfishness. When you're on the road promoting a book, you're at the disposal of the media—as you should be— talking to anyone who'll listen about your writing and as much of your personal life as you're willing to disclose publicly. The assumption is that if someone asked, you'd put on a rubber trout suit and do a little tap dance, and maybe you would, but the fishing itself seems too important to be trifled with. I'm not above taking a single evening out of a weeklong fishing trip to do a signing at a local fly shop, but my policy now is never to try to fish on a full-blown book tour.

I know that sounds unreasonably stern and it does sting to turn down some of the offers, but in order to stay relatively sane and happy and hold onto my self-respect, I've had to put things in their proper categories and try my best to keep them there:

Publishing is an actual business with contracts, deadlines, and paychecks. It may be somewhat less than perfect from a writer's point of view, but it's the only way to reach readers unless you want to be like those dissident Russian poets under Communism who had to mimeograph their poems and pass them out for free on street corners.

Writing is either a craft or an art (depending on how it goes on any given day), and although it's done in temperamental solitude, it's still an attempt at communication, so with any luck the finished product has a public face.

Fishing is an idle pastime, a sport, an observance, or a way of life, depending on who does it. It could be a metaphor for something larger or, more likely, just what it appears to be. But whatever it is, it's private.

Every once in a while, I'm introduced at some event as a "professional fly fisherman" and have to point out that I'm actually a professional *writer*, if only because no one pays me to fish.

(That would be too easy.) But in the long run, I try not to concern myself too much with job descriptions. All I know is that with the capable help of an agent, some editors and publishers, and a sympathetic accountant, I manage to make a living, although it's not exactly clear how.

Most writers have mixed feelings about promotional tours. On one hand, you're grateful to have enough of a readership to make a tour worthwhile and a publisher who'll arrange the thing and foot the bill. You remind yourself that there are writers—and you were one of them not that long ago—who would kill for this. On the other hand, you work alone, at your own pace, agonizing over every word, sentence, and paragraph, and when you're done, you'd really like the finished work to speak for itself. Andy Rooney once said of book tours, "I wrote the damned book; I don't think I should have to go out and sell it door-to-door." He said that on a book tour, if that tells you anything.

But then when I mentioned to the great landscape painter Russell Chatham that I didn't like doing book tours, he said, "Look, your readers are the people who make this wonderful little life of yours possible. The least you can do is go out and say 'hello' once in a while."

He was right on both counts: Without readers, I'd be a sixty-four-year-old dishwasher who likes to fish, and it *is* a wonderful life. There's no retirement plan, but then I've spent the last thirty-some years doing what many men have told me they want to do when *they* retire, namely, travel, fish, and write books. Also, I have too many friends with regular jobs ever to complain convincingly about having to spend a month every two or three years doing something that isn't especially fun.

And even that's not entirely true. Parts of any book tour

are excruciating, but then other parts are actually fun. I'm not a born performer, but given an engaged and responsive audience and one of those unpredictable surges of confidence, I'm capable of doing a perfectly good or even exceptional reading, and few things feel better. On the other hand, few things feel worse than putting one in the dirt, and that knowledge is the origin of stage fright. (When a true entertainer is presented with an audience, he thinks, Just let me at 'em, while the rest of us think, Oh, crap.) That's why I miss George Bush. For eight years, whenever I got a little nervous before a reading, I could say to myself, Just remember, you are a better public speaker than the president of the United States.

Like all native midwesterners, I have an inherent fear of large crowds, especially when they're looking at me expectantly. But then given the show-biz nature of book tours, I have a corresponding fear of small crowds or no crowd at all. It can happen, and when it does, you tell yourself the bookstore didn't advertise the signing or maybe there was a big game on TV that night. It never enters your mind that no one was interested enough to come. Nick Lyons once told me that publishers invented book tours as a way of keeping writers humble. It works.

Interviews with newspaper, radio, and occasionally TV folk are less terrifying because you can't see the audience, so it seems as though you're just having a conversation. In fact, I sometimes get so comfortable that I forget there *is* an audience and end up saying something I wouldn't necessarily want printed or broadcast. I've now taken to propping my notebook open in front of me and writing something like, "You're on live radio, you idiot!"

Another problem with radio and TV is that you're expected to answer questions with glib, easily digested sound bites.

(Congressman Barney Frank once said, "Television is the enemy of nuance." He could have also included most radio and all but a handful of newspapers.) Once, five seconds before going on the air live, a disk jockey said to me, "Okay, just remember, this is talk radio, not an intelligent conversation." I began to understand what William Kittredge meant when he said that the lies told by the media are "truths twisted about a quarter turn." He might have added that you quickly learn to do the twisting yourself, if only to keep someone else from doing it for you.

And then there are the well-meaning but strangely left-handed things people occasionally say. A man at a book signing once told me he liked the short chapters in my books because they were just the right length to read on the toilet every morning. I thanked him and spent the rest of the evening fighting off the insistent mental picture.

There's also the possibility—or maybe even the likelihood—that you'll be seen as a cliché. You know, you're introduced to someone outside the tiny fly-fishing fraternity, but when they learn what you do, all they can think to say is, "I went fishing with my dad once when I was seven. I ate some bad tuna salad and threw up." Or my all-time favorite, "I almost caught a fish once." Another awkward moment comes when you're introduced to a nonangler by someone who feels the need to add, "This guy's famous." They say, "Really?" with a hint of skepticism in their voice, apparently thinking, How famous can he be if you had to tell me?

It's also possible to end up in what you suddenly realize is the wrong place. I was once scheduled to sign books at the grand opening of a chain sporting goods store. The customers were all fine, upstanding Americans, but they were duck hunters and conventional bass fishers who had heard of fly fishing but weren't particularly interested in it and of course had no idea who I was. On that particular day, for one day only, the store was giving away cheap plastic duck calls to all children under twelve, so I got to sit alone behind a pile of my books for two hours listening to hundreds of hyperactive kids blowing hundreds of duck calls at the top of their lungs. But by now I'm a trouper, and I got through it by indulging in an elaborate fantasy about strangling my publicist.

There are also some purely logistical pitfalls to book tours, including incessant travel on a tight schedule and bad food, both of which can have cumulative effects. There's nothing you can do about the constant running around, but with a little effort and forethought you can avoid eating like a stray dog, although it's also possible to drift too far in the opposite direction. For one reason or another, I sometimes find myself in restaurants that bill themselves as "stylish and innovative" and that serve what some refer to as *cuisine minceur,* which is French for "real good food but not enough of it to feed a hamster." Meals like that are a treat—especially when someone else is picking up the tab—but I usually have to stop for a burger on the way back to the hotel.

Speaking of hotels, my publisher puts up writers in some pretty good ones, often the kind with a uniformed doorman and a concierge you can call to do things like print the boarding pass for your next flight and have it delivered to your room. For a guy who's used to "doing for himself," as my grandmother would have said, it's weird and not altogether comfortable to live better on the road than you do at home, but given the special circumstances, you can get used to it.

The most useful luxury is that the publisher hires a driver to take me around to signings and interviews in bigger cities. This is standard procedure for book tours. Apparently, writers can't always be trusted to find their way around one strange city after another, and when they're left unsupervised, some have been known to panic and either hole up in a bar for days on end or just go home.

These people are actually called "author escorts" rather than drivers, and they deftly handle all sorts of complicated and important details, but almost all of them are women, so there can be misunderstandings. Once, in a fly shop on the West Coast, I introduced an attractive young woman as my escort, and the guy took me aside and said, "Dude, they're treatin' you good." When I tried to explain the situation, he said, "Sure, man, whatever you say," although to his credit he didn't actually wink.

One of the oddest things about book tours for me is just spending time in cities. I don't have anything against cities; I'm just unused to them, and my personal view of reality is anchored in the sleepy, rural Midwest circa 1955. But once I relax into the noise and bustle, the odd details of the big world can be fascinating.

I saw my first and last Humvee stretch limousine in Seattle. It was in front of a restaurant unloading a bunch of people who were either rock musicians or a delegation from another dimension.

In a hotel room in San Francisco, the bedside table drawer held the usual Gideon Bible as well as a copy of *The Teachings of the Compassionate Buddha*, and out on the street I passed an old, white-haired shoe-shine guy staring dolefully at all the tennis shoes and sandals passing his stand.

I stayed at an elegant old barn of a hotel in Vermont that was built in 1769. I was already beginning to wish I was back home in Colorado, and it was an odd thought that when this thing was built they didn't even know Colorado was out here.

And in a hotel room in Portland, Oregon, I found a complimentary "uni-sex intimacy kit," the contents of which I'll leave to your imagination.

These are all things I don't see around home, and taken together they give the whole enterprise a feeling of goofy unreality, which is just as well. If I dwelled too much on what I was doing—not fishing for weeks on end while talking about it incessantly—I could begin to unravel. Still, there's a moment on every book tour when I start thinking about finding another line of work so I never have to do this again.

I deal with that by promising myself that I'll go fishing the first full day I'm home regardless of the weather or the condition of the streams, even though I know from past experience that I'll spend that day on the back porch watching the bird feeders to see what springtime migrators have arrived while I was gone and soaking up bird songs after weeks of traffic noise. (I live on a dead-end mountain road, so any car that passes either belongs here or they're lost.)

I'm seeing migrators because in recent years my books have all been released in the spring, the publisher's reasoning being that that's when the fishing seasons start. I've tried to explain that few fishermen celebrate opening day by running out and buying a book, but so far the message hasn't gotten through.

Of course, the trouble with spring book tours is that they're scheduled during the last and best of the prerunoff fishing back home, after which my local freestone streams will be too high and muddy to fly-fish for a month to six weeks. On the last tour, I met a guy in Seattle who had recently moved from Colorado and still had contacts there. He said he'd heard from a friend that the fishing where I live was real good right then, but that runoff would probably be on by the time I got home. I'm sure he was trying to be helpful.

Oddly enough, though, the biggest problem with book tours is that you can begin to feel overappreciated, which is something few of us have a strategy to deal with. Most of the people you meet in the normal course of things seem deeply interested in you, although in some cases that's just their job. Also, the people who show up for your signings often say they like your books, but before you start getting cocky, you have to remind yourself that the people who *don't* like your books seldom line up to have them autographed. You resolve to keep your head on straight and succeed most of the time, but eventually you spend so much time talking about yourself that you begin to think you must be a pretty intriguing guy.

With all that attention, the temptation to pose is almost irresistible. The chances of seeing any of these people again are slim, so you can either be who you are or you can briefly become who you wish you were: the heroic outdoorsman, the brooding writer, or the dispenser of Zen-like wisdom. It's the same impulse that causes a middle-aged cat food salesman to confess to the pretty stranger in the seat next to him on a flight to Houston that he's really a secret agent.

It's all kind of fun in an exhausting, hyperextended sort of way, but when it's finally over, it's a relief to get back home where your friends are happy enough that you've found honest work, but know you too well to be overly impressed.

9

DECKERS

I drove down to fish the South Platte River on what was predicted to be a relatively warm January day before the next Arctic cold front blew in. It wasn't supposed to be all *that* warm—just a little warmer than it had been or was expected to be for at least the next week—and as it turned out, the projected high in the low forties was just a cruel hoax by the National Weather Service. Still, it was the only apparent window on the river for the foreseeable future and I was getting desperate.

For one thing, I hadn't been fishing in a month because of the weather. It had snapped cold back before Christmas and, uncharacteristically for Colorado, it had stayed that way. One bitter storm after another marched through with record-breaking snowfalls in the mountains and none of the usual thaws in between that would let a guy run down to the river for a day to shake off the shack nasties. Normally, this is one of the many places on earth where you can say, "If you don't like the weather, just wait a day," and weeks of monotonously identical cold days had become weirdly oppressive.

The South Platte is about a two-hour drive from home and it's my only close shot at fishing in a hard winter. It's a good, strong tailwater that stays open for miles while the streams closer to home are either frozen or too low and bone-chilling to fish. That includes our own local tailwater which, for complicated reasons, ices up bank-to-bank except for a few hundred yards below the dam, but that short stretch is usually too crowded with despondent fly casters and trout made hysterical by the sight of a hundred flies a day.

There are other, more distant tailwaters than the Platte, but they involve longer drives through the mountains in risky weather, multiple days on the river to make the trip worthwhile, the expense of motel rooms because it's too shitty to camp, and so on. You shoot for one of those periodic midwinter thaws when daytime temperatures can get up near 50 for two or three days running, but those are often caused by strong, bone-dry Chinook winds that can melt two feet of snow from the top down, leaving dry ground underneath, and that blow at near hurricane force and make fly casting an insane exercise. But then just the possibility of going fishing somewhere means that eventually you *have* to go. In theory, I'm delighted that the fishing season in Colorado never closes. In practice, a closed season could make life easier.

So my friends and I compulsively checked the weather on the South Platte at the little crossroads town of Deckers and called each other with the forecasts. The town is roughly seventy miles south of here as the crow flies and only about 400 feet higher in elevation, but it's in a deeper, darker valley, and the rule of thumb is that if it's cold here, with nighttime lows around 10 degrees, it's worse there at more like 10 or more *below*. It's no accident that near the bottom end of the Cheesman Canyon stretch there's a long, slow pool known as the Icebox.

That's how things stood when the mailman delivered the long cardboard tube that contained my new Walter Babb bamboo fly rod. I'd almost ordered one of Walter's rods on the spot when we fished together in Tennessee the previous spring but decided to give myself a cooling off period to ponder a few things. Jamaica Kincaid once said, "If there's something you really love, you should have more than just one or two of them." True enough, but I still had more than enough fly rods already and, as reasonable as Walter's prices were, I wasn't made of money.

But then what *is* money anyway? Isn't it just symbolic value that comes in hard and goes out easy? You spend most of it on necessary but mundane stuff like gasoline, utilities, insurance, and new tires for the truck: the interminable dreariness of bills that can begin to look like the entire meaning of life. There's always some benefit there—though usually less than there should be for the price—it's just that it's not *fun*.

You can see where this was headed. I held out for a week or so after I got home, then called Walter to order a seven-foot nine-inch, 4-weight built on a modified Payne taper that I knew I wouldn't see until fall at the earliest.

Walter called in November to say he was "fixin' to start on the rod." When it finally arrived in late December, I dry-cast it out in the yard on an 18-degree afternoon until my hands went numb. It was sweet, but casting is one thing and fishing is another, so I waited for the break in the weather that would let me get to the river until my patience finally ran out.

I checked with Danny Brennan at the Flies & Lies fly shop in Deckers and learned that it didn't look good. The river was flowing at forty cubic feet per second—barely a trickle—and nighttime temperatures had been in the neighborhood of 20 below, so there was deep, crusty snow, wide shelves of bank ice surrounding narrow, open channels, and lots of slush in the water. (You can count on Danny for an honest fishing report.) On the bright side, the trout were pooled up in the low water, so at least you could find them.

I got to the river at about nine-thirty the next morning and took all the time I needed and more to bundle up and rig the new rod, stopping twice to sit in the heated cab of the pickup drinking coffee from the thermos. The sky was darkly overcast, and I guessed the air temperature in the high teens, with enough of a breeze to really sting.

I had layered myself from the skin out with cotton, flannel, wool, and fleece, topped off with a GORE-TEX windbreaker, fingerless gloves, and an insulated hat with earflaps. I'd also laced my wading boots loosely to leave more loft in my wool socks for extra warmth. (I'm sensitive to this because I once frostbit a couple of toes. I didn't lose them, but they temporarily turned a disturbing purple color, and ever since they've been the first things to get cold and the last to warm up.) Loose boots actually do keep your feet a little warmer, but they also make you more likely to stumble. Like everything else about winter fly fishing, it's six of one and a half dozen of the other.

There were two other cars parked ahead of me at the turnout and only three other fishermen spread out in that normally crowded half mile of river. We'd all thought the same thing that morning: that if you're willing to fish in the poorest conditions, you can have more water to yourself on these famous rivers, but then once you get there you remember that there's a reason why they call them "poor conditions." I'd called two friends to see if they wanted to come with me that day, but after checking the weather report they both decided they were too busy and I idly wondered if they were the smart ones.

There's a certain long, deep run above the Deckers bridge that I had my eye on because it always holds lots of fish and would be one of the few prime spots in these low flows. (If you're familiar with the river, you know where it is; if not, I won't spill the beans.) Anyway, there was a guy already fishing it, so I fooled around waiting for him to get tired, cold, or frustrated enough to leave.

I fished a long, straight run of pocket water fifty yards downstream, where I could keep him in sight without appearing to hover, although of course he knew what I was up to. It goes without saying that it's never permissible to crowd another fisherman—never mind that some people do it anyway—but I think it's okay to present yourself at a polite distance as the guy who's next in line for the spot. On the other side of the equation, if you're there first you *do* have squatter's rights, but that falls somewhere short of actually owning the pool.

So I blind-fished the pocket water downstream, killing time at first and then getting into it. I managed to spot two rainbows in a good-sized plunge pool and cast methodically to them. The smaller one mouthed my nymph, but I missed him. The bigger one finally got tired of me and swam away. I'd been casting to that second fish from an ice shelf, and when I went to move, I found that my wet felt-soled boots had frozen in place, although not permanently.

I finally ran into the guy from the pool as we were both heading back to our cars to warm up, and I asked him how he did. "I got two pretty much by accident," he said, "but there was so much slush in the water it was almost pointless." The man wore a pained expression that had nothing to do with the number of trout he'd caught, and his nose was red while the rest of his face was a bloodless gray. He looked as cold as I felt. He showed me the two nymphs he'd been using, but they were encased in ice, so I couldn't make them out very well. It would have been pleasant to stand there and talk for a while the way you can do on a slow day on a nearly vacant river, but we were both too cold for that.

The guy broke down his rod before getting in his car, but he didn't take off his waders, so I guessed he wasn't giving up and going home, but moving to another spot that was too far away to walk. After letting his engine warm up for five minutes, he pulled out slowly and headed back downstream, skidding sideways a little in the packed snow.

I'd seen the other two fishermen leave earlier, so I had the leisure to rest the pool for half an hour while running my heater full blast and drinking coffee that was by then just lukewarm. I knew there'd be hot, if not necessarily fresh, coffee down at the fly shop, but caving in to that temptation would put me a step closer to giving up entirely, and it was too early to start losing my nerve.

When I got down to the pool, the slush situation wasn't as bad as the guy had described it, meaning he'd either been whining a little, or, more likely, that things had changed in the last forty-five minutes. There was still plenty of slush in the water, but for the time being most of it hugged the far bank with the current, leaving better than half the pool on the inside open.

There were a few smaller trout strung out in the shallow tail with more and bigger fish toward the deeper eye of the pool, which is the usual configuration for this spot: fish stacked according to size from the worst to the best feeding lies. They weren't in what you'd call a feeding frenzy, but they were suspended off the bottom a little, and now and then one would dodge to the side or elevate slightly to eat an errant bug. That meant I had a shot. You can almost always spot fish in this river—especially when the flow is down—but as often as not in the winter they're sitting motionless on the bottom and the only way you know they're not dead is that they're not upside down.

This is a notorious small fly river in the winter (if not year-round) so I put on a light twist of lead and a pair of Midge Pupa patterns—a size 24 and a 26, one dark, one light. I now carry 3X magnifier glasses in order to see these little bitty things and a pair of needle-nosed tweezers so I can get them out of the box with cold fingers. I even fashioned a clumsy tweezer holster on the midge box out of duct tape, but the design needs work. So far, I haven't dropped the tweezers in the river, but it's only a matter of time.

In order to keep the guides from freezing, I fished a short length of line that I was careful not to either shoot or retrieve and added weight incrementally as I worked up toward the deeper head of the pool. It was slow going. Every ten casts or so, the part of the line that was wet would ice up in a pattern resembling a string of pearls and I'd have to chip it off before I could cast again. By the time that was done, a glaze of clear ice would have formed around the wet flies. I thought it would probably melt away once the hooks were back in the water, but I wasn't certain of that, so I'd chip them free with my thumbnail. Then I'd have to stop and warm my fingers in my armpits for a while.

I've repeatedly promised myself that I won't fish if it's so windy I can't keep my hat on or so cold the line freezes, but most years I end up doing both a few times anyway, sometimes by accident and occasionally on purpose because, as Annie Dillard said, "Tomorrow is another day only up to a point."

Of course, every time I took a break I'd start thinking about the heater in the truck parked no more than seventy-five yards away, but then it was the proximity of relief that let me stay where I was. If I'd been upstream in the canyon with a mile or more to go to get out, I'd have already been walking back or building a fire. As it was, I was oddly happy in the hellish sort of way winter fishermen become used to. In fact, most stories about winter fishing center on how cold it was. A friend recently told me he got so cold fishing the Frying Pan River one January that he could have cut glass with his nipples, but he didn't mention whether or not he'd caught anything.

I'm sure it's just my midwestern upbringing, but I think being too cold makes you feel more immediately alive than almost any other nonlethal extreme I can think of. Cold forces you to confront actual reality instead of what someone once called "the usual rehearsal of abstractions." Life becomes as simple as it is uncomfortable, and there's the thought that assigning meaning to reality and peeling away layers of meaning so reality herself can breathe amount to the same procedure. Your ambitions are reduced to catching a trout or two and then going to warm up. Larger considerations of sex, mortality, money, and career can wait until the feeling returns to your extremities.

There's also a kind of perverse pride in the idea that this is something anyone *could* do, but that not everyone *would,* which reminds me of those old Swedish guys I remember from my childhood in Minnesota who would celebrate the new year by chopping a hole in the ice on the nearest lake and jumping naked into the freezing water. Reporters never tired of wanting to know why, but the interviews were understandably brief and usually disappointing. Clearly, these guys had gotten beyond asking themselves that question or trying to answer it for anyone who didn't already get it. I never had the guts to try it myself, but it was my first hint, at about age thirteen, that not being taken seriously could be a kind of saving grace. And of course the reporters always left too early, recording the spectacle but missing the fact that the real celebration came later with central heating, schnapps, and bratwurst.

I don't know how long I fished the pool. It seemed like a long time, but cold fishing time is subjective and I hadn't looked at my pocket watch since I got to the river. After that it was buried under so many layers of clothing and waders that I might as well have left it at home. I felt okay about hogging the spot because the three fishermen who'd been there that morning had all left and no one had come along to take their place. As far as I knew, I had the whole river to myself.

I usually try to avoid the implied competitiveness of keeping score, but on a day when all indications pointed to a miserable skunk and I got some anyway, I can't quite forget that I missed two trout in that pool and landed seven. The last one was a fourteen-inch rainbow hooked by accident while I was casting to a much bigger fish I could just make out holding deep in the tub at the head of the pool. It was one of those tricky drifts where the current wants to pull the flies out and away, while the weight wants to pull them down and in. I thought I knew where my flies were, but the trout I hooked was three feet to the left of the one I was casting to.

I played the smaller fish downstream so as not to spook the big one, and made a point of giving him his due. He was a fat, handsome rainbow that put up a good fight on a light bamboo rod and 7x tippet, and I didn't want to be disappointed by him even though he wasn't the one I was after.

Back at the spot, it took a few minutes of staring into the water to convince myself that the big trout wasn't there anymore and that it wouldn't have mattered anyway because in the space of just a few minutes the water had filled with slush. It must have warmed up a little: not enough to make me *feel* any warmer, but just enough above freezing for more bank ice to calve into the current, making the water not only opaque, but pretty much unfishable, even with a heavily weighted nymph rig. I'd spent most of the day wishing it was warmer, but I hadn't foreseen the consequence of a slush hatch, proving once again that what seems like misery can later turn out to be luck you didn't recognize at the time.

The rest is anticlimax. Back at the truck, I left my rod in the rack and my waders on while I blasted the heater and gnawed on my sandwich: a gut bomb I'd bought at the last minute at a gas station in Conifer consisting of two slices of tasteless white bread around a vaguely egg-salad–like substance. My thermos was ice-cold and it was past three by the dashboard clock, so there'd be no more hot coffee at the fly shop. Danny closes up at three in the winter so he can fish for a few hours before dark or, on a day like this, go home and start a fire in the woodstove.

I was still a little too keyed up to go home myself, so I drove downstream to see how much of the river had stayed open. A lot of it, actually—all the way down past the bridge at Trumbull—except by then it was choked with so much slush that the current had slowed to the consistency of syrup and an icy tinkle reminiscent of a gin and tonic had joined the usual quiet rush of the river. The forecast was for colder weather, but I didn't know then that within a few days the low at Deckers would reach 33 below zero and the river would freeze solid from bank to bank, something no one I know had ever seen or heard of before.

I derigged at a turnout below a spot known as the Beaver Pool and began mentally composing a letter to Walter. All rod makers like favorable reports, but I know some who'd be offended to learn that I'd been chucking lead between ice shelves with their elegant little bamboo dry fly rod. But then Walter is nothing if not practical and I didn't think he'd mind.

10

A SMALL RIVER

There's a small river in Wyoming that I've floated off and on with friends probably for more years than I'd guess, since lately the actual passage of time has gotten ahead of my perception of it. The river drops steeply from seeps and snowfields near the Continental Divide to around 7,000 feet through tundra, spruce, and fir forest and foothills pinewoods. From there it meanders out across cottonwood bottom country, then finally steps down through the kind of rim rock and juniper canyon where you wouldn't be surprised to see a mountain lion licking its paws on a flat rock. That's a drop of around 6,000 feet in elevation and five complete life zones—from alpine to high plains—in the space of less than a hundred miles, which isn't that unusual in the Rocky Mountains, where environments are often foreshortened by altitude.

Most of the drainage is worth fishing, including the tributaries, but the real sweet spot is the dozen or so miles of cottonwood and canyon before it enters a much larger river at a surprisingly undramatic confluence pool. The first time I fished this bottom end was with my friends Chris Schrantz and Vince Zounek right after Chris called unexpectedly one late June. After guiding in the area for several seasons, he'd sniffed out the timing on a stretch of this river that most visiting fishermen overlooked and that many others thought was more trouble than it was worth because of access problems. He said the runoff was dropping quickly and there was a narrow window— probably less than a week—but if we could drive up on short notice, he might be able to show us "a nice little Green Drake hatch." Years of guiding and his natural midwestern reticence have trained Chris to underreport rather than sensationalize, so this was a better review than you might think.

That first day, the three of us floated in Chris's thirteen-foot raft. This boat is really only big enough for two and it seemed even smaller than usual because Vince is a big guy, but when the river is down to fishable flows, there are places where a small inflatable with a shallow draft is the most you can stuff down it.

The weather that day was the kind trout, mayflies, and fishermen all like for their own reasons. It was warm, but not downright hot, with a high overcast to cut the usual bright sun and about as calm as it ever gets in Wyoming. The wind in this state is famously unrelenting. Native fly fishers shy away from 2-weight rods and learn to cast with the same stroke they'd use to split firewood or drive nails. So whatever else happens, getting a day that's only breezy is akin to winning the lottery.

The Drakes started on schedule at about ten in the morning and more or less poured off the river under a pearl-colored sky till midafternoon. Chris already had this wired before he called, so we launched early enough to float downstream and hit the beginning of the hatch in the best water. I won't guess how many rainbows, browns, and the odd cuttbow we boated, but I'll say the better fish were between sixteen and eighteen inches long, and a few might have cracked twenty, although in the excitement we didn't bother to measure them.

After the hatch petered out, we reeled in and took our time floating the last few miles down to the takeout, wolfing sandwiches because we'd forgotten to eat lunch, and watching the banks scroll by at a walking pace. We all say we fish in part because of the beautiful places it takes us, but casting dry flies from a moving boat requires the kind of concentration that doesn't allow for much sightseeing. As someone once said, when the fishing gets furious, the river you see is like a slide show run by a speed freak.

Fishing is like any other quest in the sense that when you finally close the deal, you can be at a loss about what to do next. The hatch had lasted for hours, but once it was over, dozens of trout and miles of river seemed to have gone by entirely too fast. I think we all understood that by the time we were trailering up the raft at the takeout, we'd be wondering if we'd appreciated this as much as we should have, and that by the time we were digging into dinner specials at the Mangy Moose Café, the memory would already be yellowing around the edges.

There was also the danger that when we were asked about this later, we'd automatically dredge up one of those unfortunate macho clichés that have infected the sport. Someone asks, "How was it?" and you puff up to your full height and say, "We kicked ass and took names," as if your goal was to rid the world of trout. Sadly, almost nothing one fisherman says to another quite conveys the message, so there was the possibility that we wouldn't talk about this much, partly to keep the secret, but mostly because it was sort of personal.

We did the same float again the next day and came as close as possible to repeating the performance after burning off the novelty of it the day before. The hatch came off and we caught fish, although maybe not as many as we think, since after certain great days you can exaggerate convincingly even to yourself and a couple of eyewitnesses. To be honest, the trout were eager and gullible and the fishing was pretty easy. We all have unreasonably high opinions of our skills, but as a friend says, there are days when a chimpanzee could catch fish.

It all went so smoothly the first time that the difficulty of hitting this right didn't register until subsequent seasons when we floated the river but didn't find the Drakes or planned to float but didn't because it was either too high and cold for the hatch or too skinny to float the raft. It turns out that in most normal seasons there are only about three weeks sometime in late June to early July when the water has dropped and warmed enough for the Drakes to come off. There are also roughly three weeks after the runoff when it's still high enough to float a raft, but those two times don't always coincide or even overlap.

Being able to float is crucial because the land along most of this stretch is private. In Wyoming that means that the actual water in the river belongs to the People, but not the banks or the bottom or anything attached to either. So you can float and fish legally, but you can't walk or wade or beach your boat or drop an anchor. Technically, you're trespassing if your raft so much as bumps a rock, and since landowners here are proprietary about their river, they tend to *get* technical. There's the story of a fisherman who took a trespassing bust for grabbing a tree branch from a raft in order to untangle his fly. That's such a pat cautionary tale that you could wonder if it's even true, although it does make the point.

I'm told that a few decades ago things were more casual. Back then the occasional raft was rowed by a neighbor having a few beers, putting a few trout on a stringer and barely making a dent. No big deal. Then some guides got wind of it—just one or two at first, then more as word leaked out—but they held it close to their vests. They'd float it now and then during the few weeks when conditions were right, either with friends on their rare days off or maybe with the odd client who wouldn't insist on a sure thing. The river did get fished, but not enough to affect the size and number of trout or to educate the fish. It was still possible to do an entire float without seeing another boat on the water or another trailer at the put-in.

But even then, as you floated from public water into private, there was a large sign laying out the detailed riot act about trespassing. The first time I saw it, it seemed unnecessarily menacing, but then it's easier to stand up for public access when you're the beneficiary. If I owned the land around an obscure and nearly perfect trout river, would I post signs saying PUBLIC FISH-ING—EVERYONE WELCOME? All I know for sure is that if I did I'd have to have the signs custom-made because nothing like that is available off the rack.

It probably goes without saying that I didn't see that Drake hatch again for something like a decade, give or take a season or two. There were the years when we tried and failed and the years when it was pointless to try. Eventually, the difficul-ties became a running joke as well as the source of the river's peculiar charm. At the same time that you'd curse the thing for its impossible timing, you had to admire a fishery that protects itself so efficiently.

Of course, there are a few other opportunities. Earlier in the season there's said to be a stonefly hatch that's even less depend-able than the Drakes, and in higher water you can always dredge nymphs and streamers, but both are considered to be shots in the dark. In the long run, the river goes largely unfished for most of every year, so it's unlikely to ever get pounded to death as so many have.

It should also go without saying that a few things have changed in the intervening years. For one thing, Chris now builds drift boats for a living and no longer guides except for the odd charity gig, but he's held on to his local contacts and keeps an eye on this little river from a distance. The campground where we rent rooms in a subdivided double-wide trailer known as the Brown Palace changed hands and the price went up, but not so much that it isn't still cheap. And Vince now owns his own thirteen-foot raft, so with him and me in one raft and Chris and his boat-building partner Andy in the other, everyone finally has enough elbow room.

The last time we floated it, there were also more boats on the river than there used to be. Not exactly a crowd, just *some* boats where we could remember none—a sure sign of a secret beginning to leak air. The way one man tells it, the gentleman's agreement among guides lasted for years, but, inevitably, one guy started running a few too many trips, others saw money being made that could have been theirs, and the deal unraveled. Also, some clients aren't as clueless as guides like to think, and it doesn't take an enormous leap of logic to come back with your own raft and do the same float for free.

Of course, the real danger here doesn't come from a few extra boats on the water. It comes from those inevitable few who glance up from the fishing long enough to see not silent pastures surrounding groves of cottonwoods, but luxury home sites for the next generation of CEOs. And if you think ranchers can be snarky, you've never dealt with new money.

The demands of politeness on small water are obvious to anyone who's familiar with float fishing and whose mother taught them manners, so there were few traffic problems, but there *was* the occasional whiff of xenophobic tension. Nothing overt, just the odd hairy eyeball or pointedly unreturned wave. That's partly just a function of more people, but it's also because some of us on the river are Colorado fly fishers, who are known in certain circles as out-of-state fun hogs with no clue and an unearned sense of entitlement. (That's a direct quote.)

One evening as we were walking back to our campground after supper, a pickup stopped in the middle of the deserted road and the driver yelled, "Hey, you hippies! Get outta town!" inducing a collective flashback among the four of us. It turned out to be an old guide friend of Chris's having a little homemade fun. The gag was funny precisely because under slightly different circumstances it might not have been.

There's probably no way around this kind of thing, since the places that attract fishermen eventually end up attracting too many of us, and in larger numbers we do have an annoying tendency to piss in the whiskey. I've lived for over thirty years in the shadow of Rocky Mountain National Park and understand that although visitors contribute to the local economy, that doesn't mean we're always overjoyed to see them. It's the same scenario by which an exterminator can make his livelihood from cockroaches without actually *liking* cockroaches. Meanwhile, the original logic of the regional culture is bypassed in the usual direction of jackalope mounts and rubber tomahawks.

An old college friend of mine may have stumbled on a solution. He disappeared for the better part of a quarter century (that kind of thing happened in the 1960s) and finally resurfaced as a bona fide desert rat living simply and happily in the blistering middle of nowhere. I've never been a desert guy myself, but it made a kind of sense. Maybe the answer is to find a place that's beautiful in such a left-handed way that it would kill your average tourist in twelve hours—either from exposure or boredom—and then learn to love it. But then few of us actually get to choose what we love. In some familiar but still gut-wrenching way, the choice is made for us.

All that notwithstanding, the last trip happened the way it always does. There was the call from Chris; the hasty arrangements; the drive up with Chris, Andy, Vince, and me towing two rafts piggy-backed on a drift boat trailer; then checking into the Brown Palace with three of us in one room and Vince alone in another so he could snore in peace and the rest of us could sleep.

The flow was right, the water was clear, and the first run down the river was the usual journey of rediscovery. The shape of the channel hasn't changed appreciably since I first saw it, but every year the same spring flood that pushes aside old sweepers and strainers also drops new trees into the river, so although the place is now entirely familiar, you still don't know what's coming next.

This time what had once been a gentle bend had become a suicidal chute into a gnarly root ball, followed immediately by an obstacle course of bleached limbs. At another spot, a mature broad-leaf cottonwood had fallen completely across the river, with the root ball on one bank, the crown resting on the other, and the trunk suspended a foot above the water. The leaves were still bright green and supple, meaning it had happened very recently or that the tree had kept just enough of its roots in the ground to survive like that for years. There's a similar cottonwood near where I live. It blew over one winter in an eighty-mile-an-hour Chinook wind and has flourished for the last twenty-some years lying on its back, making the best of the hand it was dealt.

Vince and I tried to squeeze the raft under the trunk, but it wouldn't fit, so we dragged it thirty yards around on the bank. The fully loaded raft weighs over three hundred pounds, and it's a clumsy load, so we rested on the other side watching a robin catch Green Drakes until we caught our breath, but no longer. The one loophole in the otherwise iron-clad trespass rule is that you can get out to portage around obstacles, but it's best not to dawdle in case a landowner happens by.

And there was the spot where a muscular current did its best to push us into a bank that had an old but still serviceable barbed-wire fence embedded in it that could have gutted the raft like a fish. We spotted it too late, so it was a closer call than it had to be, but Vince pulled hard and we missed it by an inch. Ninety percent of rowing in current is finesse and forethought, but for that other 10 percent, it's good to have a big strong man on the oars.

The Drakes started coming off around eleven o'clock—an hour later than usual because of the bright sun. The hatch was sparse at first, but built quickly to where there were more than enough bugs to get the fish going, but not so many that they wouldn't pick out your fly. Drakes are a big event for the fish— day after day of big, easy meals—and they give rise to the belief among fishermen that even trout, with their tiny little reptilian brains, can be happy.

On the long drive home, we'd have time to ponder the question that weighs heavily on fishermen when they're away from the water. Namely: Is the river as good as it used to be? (The inevitable answer is "Yes and no—and what difference does it make?") But at the moment, we were too busy dodging dead-falls and catching fish to worry about that.

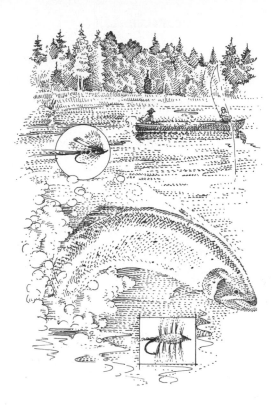

11

ATLANTIC SALMON

The adventure began when my fly rods turned up missing. I'd flown from Denver to Bangor, Maine, via New York to meet Jim Babb, but for unknown reasons Delta Airlines decided to fly my rods to Boston instead. When I asked how they'd managed to lose my rods with only one connecting flight, the woman behind the baggage counter cheerfully corrected me. "They're not *lost*," she said, pointing at a computer screen, "They're in *Boston*," a purely technical distinction that I didn't find helpful.

She said not to worry, that it was their policy to deliver side-tracked luggage whenever it came in, and since Bangor is still a relatively small and friendly airport, she even introduced me to the guy who drove the delivery van. But when they learned that by the time the next flight from Boston arrived, we'd be an eight- or nine-hour drive north, in the Miramichi Valley in New Brunswick, Canada, their confidence began to wither. When we added that we'd be at a private Atlantic salmon camp down a monkey puzzle of unmarked logging roads that not even Jim and I were sure we could find—not to mention halfway across the province from the nearest airport—it began to dawn on all of us simultaneously that I'd be fishing with borrowed tackle. I left with a claim number and a solemn promise that my rods would be waiting for me when I came through Bangor on the return trip.

It could have been worse. Jim is a lifelong fisherman with a stack of fly rods that resembles a cord of firewood, so I had my pick of what was left after he'd packed his own gear. I ended up with a two-handed fourteen-foot 8-weight that felt perfectly good except that it wasn't my own beloved spey rod, but I resolved not to get into a snit about it. Lately, I'd been telling myself that fishing tackle—among other things—was just stuff, and here was my karmic opportunity to cowboy up.

Jim and I spent the next day driving up, with minimal stops for gas and coffee, and hit the ground running when we got to the camp. (Normal people tend to kick back and relax a little at the end of a long drive, but fishermen seldom qualify for that benefit.) There were some quick introductions and a brief look around, and then we hustled into waders, strung up rods, and hit the river with a few hours of daylight left.

The Sevogle River, a major tributary of the Miramichi, was

running clear, but it was tea-colored and a little too high to fish well, though not quite high enough to make fishing pointless. That wasn't the best news I've heard at the beginning of a fishing trip, but it wasn't the worst, either. Neither of us got a pull that evening, but no one thought anything of a few fishless hours, since Atlantic salmon are famous for coming days, weeks, or even months apart, if at all. We were just getting the feel of a new river and keeping our hooks in the water, which is the first rule of salmon fishing.

Drinks and hors d'oeuvres started at about seven. Dinner began at nine and was still going strong seven courses and multiple bottles of wine later at a little after midnight, or two hours past my normal bedtime. When I excused myself going on one o'clock, someone said there was no need to get up early because fishing didn't start till late morning. I could guess why.

What I'm calling a "camp"—because that's what you call it in this part of the world—was actually a small, privately owned estate carved out of second-growth boreal forest for the single-minded purpose of living well while fishing for salmon. It consisted of the rambling main house, assorted outbuildings, and a smaller, matching house for the owner's personal staff: the chef, an assistant, and his camp manager and guide. There were also roughly two acres of perfectly mown bluegrass lawn and a swimming pool, both of which looked incongruous in the great north woods.

The place was owned by a man Jim described as "unnecessarily wealthy," and I was there by virtue of being the friend Jim was told he could bring when he got the invitation. Of course, all Jim had told me on the phone was that the fishing was good and that the accommodations might be a cut or two above my usual program of looking for a cheap motel and a passable café.

As it turned out, I was so unused to this level of luxury that I had to be filled in on some of the finer points. The foie gras one night was said to be excellent, but it just tasted like goose liver to me. Jim also told me the wines served with dinner were the kind you only read about. I wouldn't have known because I don't read about them, and even in my drinking days I didn't have the palate or the wallet for wine.

When Jim finally got around to asking me what I thought of the place—with a hint of mischievous grin on his face—I said it was nice, but it probably wouldn't be the way I'd spend my own fortune if I had one. Deadpan western populism meets laconic Down East humor. I'd call it a tie.

The camp manager was a compact, weathered-looking man known as Frenchy who has guided for Atlantic salmon on the Miramichi drainage since the age of sixteen and has now come in out of the cold in middle age to be the owner's personal guide. In some circles, the nickname "Frenchy" is the Canuck version of "Bubba," but when your full name is Michael French, your fate is pretty much sealed at birth.

Frenchy is brash, funny, confident, and profoundly opinionated in the forgivable way of someone who actually knows what he's doing. He was consumed early by salmon, never looked back, and quickly became one of those harmless misfits you see in fishing who do no appreciable damage to the world at large and in the end have only cost themselves the normal life that they never wanted anyway.

Late the next morning, we drove to the parking lot of a convenience store in the nearest town to meet Betty, the Mi'kmaq guide who would take us fishing on the First Nation reserve. Frenchy had arranged this by phone the day before. He thought the fishing might be better on the Little Southwest Miramichi but couldn't take us there himself because only natives can guide on the reserve and nonresidents can't fish anywhere in New Brunswick without a guide. (Whether this law is intended to bolster the local economy or save bumbling foreigners from themselves is a question no one seemed willing to answer.) He said he didn't think Betty was much of a guide but that she'd have to do. Jim told me later that as far as Frenchy was concerned, anyone who wasn't Frenchy couldn't be much of a guide.

The day was gray and chilly, and although the rain wasn't what you'd call a downpour, it was steady and persistent. Good dank, sloppy fishing weather. The Little Southwest was running high enough to flood a few inches of bank-side grass, and the long run Betty took us to looked featureless and uninteresting at first, but I started to like it better when I saw a salmon roll out in mid-current. Betty went through my fly box, didn't like what she saw, and gave me a size 6 Ally's Shrimp of her own. Some guides refuse to like your flies as a matter of professional pride, while others simply have a better idea, but it's hard to tell them apart, so I just said, "Thanks." Then Jim and I spread out and started casting.

Brian O'Keefe once said that guys who like to fish these endless, even-flowing step-and-cast runs smoke too much pot, and I'll admit that would probably have helped, but although there's lots of room for finely honed talent in salmon fishing, two of the most useful skills are thoroughness and persistence. Anyway, by the end of the day Jim had landed a couple of grilse. I'd played and lost one grilse, landed another, and got a lovely twelve-pound bright salmon that sent me to the bank to drink lukewarm coffee from the thermos and smoke a damp cigarette to commemorate the moment.

It was still raining the next morning when we went back to the same run with Betty. We parked in the same spot off a blacktop road and walked down to the river through someone's back yard, stopping to pet the chained-up husky mix we'd made friends with the day before. The rain hadn't let up, and although the water level looked the same, floating sticks and pinecones suggested it was slowly rising. We fished for nine hours, and I got one halfhearted tug. A few other heart-stoppers turned out to be tweaks from floating sticks.

By the time we got off the river, the rain had developed into a cloudburst, and we drove back to the camp through axle-deep puddles with windshield wipers slapping. A wet cow moose ran full-tilt across the road in front of us as if it were looking for shelter.

It rained hard all through dinner and was still pouring at six the next morning when Jim and I got up. We took our first cups of coffee out to the screened porch and looked at the river, which was muddy and loud and out of its banks, as we'd expected. I predicted the regulation rainy day of reading, pacing, boredom, and too much coffee in the great north woods. Jim nodded sagely. The things that can go wrong in fishing are so commonplace it's hard to think of them as actually being *wrong*. It's just how things are.

The rain had tapered off to a drizzle, and a faint slice of blue sky had appeared on the western horizon by the time Frenchy dragged in about ten o'clock with no trace of a hangover and in the best possible mood. He said these rivers drain quickly after a rain and that when they drop to half the amount they've risen, however much or little that is, the salmon bite.

"Tomorrow," he said.

The next morning, we spent some time trailering up Frenchy's beautiful old twenty-six-foot wooden Sharpe canoe. These boats were first built by Raymond Sharpe starting back in 1947, and they're still being made today under the same name, but among insiders the new boats are said not to measure up to the old ones, which have become a kind of gold standard in the region. When Frenchy brought out the anchor, I cautiously said I wouldn't have thought a twenty-pound anchor would be enough to hold such a big, heavy boat. In the tone of voice you might use on a curious six-year-old, he said, "If the small anchor won't hold, the current is too strong for salmon, so you're in the wrong place." The wisdom of the ages.

On the drive downriver, we passed a local fisherman Frenchy knew, and they had a short conversation through driver's-side pickup windows. Between some missing teeth and a thick French-Canadian accent, I couldn't make out much of what the guy said, but I did clearly hear him say that the river was "rotten with salmon."

At the put-in on the Northwest Miramichi, we met Bud, a third-generation guide whose Sharpe canoe was identical to Frenchy's but more recently refinished and tricked out with a depth finder, a tape deck, and a cell phone in a holster. Jim and Frenchy headed off together, and Bud and I motored upstream to the confluence pool where the Sevogle joins the Northwest.

The pool was a long triangle of bumpy water between the two main currents off a narrow point. Bud said it hadn't dropped quite as much as he'd hoped, but it would still be the place where salmon would stop to rest and he thought we should fish it. Once we were anchored for the first drop and Bud had dutifully tied my fly on for me, he asked, "Do you mind if I smoke?" I said, "Of course not," and he proceeded to roll himself an enormous doobie. I knew he meant marijuana. Over the last few days, I'd observed that half the people in the valley seemed to be marginally cooked on homegrown with no apparent ill effects except a healthy appetite.

The confluence pool didn't pan out after two passes with two different flies, so we motored on upstream, fished some long, riffly runs on the lower Sevogle and got into some grilse, one of which was about as big as they get. Technically, grilse are small salmon that have spent only one year at sea, as opposed to multiple years for a proper salmon. *Legally*, a grilse is no more than 63 centimeters long, or about 25½ inches. A fish of that size weighs in the neighborhood of six pounds, feels like a tensed muscle in your hands, and fights twice as hard as a trout of equal size. As someone had said the day before while we waited out the high water, salmon and grilse are saltwater fish that just happen to be in a freshwater river at the moment.

I'd never thought of it that way before, and during one of the many lulls in the conversation, I took my seventh cup of coffee out on the back porch to ponder in private. I tried to picture the forbidding North Atlantic no more than eight miles downstream and to fathom the spooky telemetry that allows a salmon swimming off the coast of Scotland to locate his home river in North America. All I could come up with was a quote from the poet Rumi, who said, "Sell your cleverness and buy bewilderment." It seemed like good advice, especially when there was no alternative.

On our last day, I got a chance to fish from the canoe with Frenchy on the main branch of the Miramichi. Some people are just fine fishermen and by all accounts (including his own) Frenchy is one of them, so I paid close attention and asked as

many questions as I could without conducting an outright inter-
rogation. Why this fly instead of that one? Why this pool and not
the one upstream?

I also tried to get a handle on fishing access. I'd learned
from the regulation booklet that large parts of the drainage
were reserved for New Brunswick residents—which seemed
fair enough—but the rest was still a puzzle. As it turns out, the
water is controlled by endless, arcane rules, some written down,
others merely understood. The oldest are tribal, while the new-
est are based on first French and then later on English common
law and date to the 1600s. Best to just do what you're told.

I should say that I'm not a very experienced Atlantic salmon
fisherman. I've done just enough of it over the last fifteen years
or so to locate the flaw in the sport for someone who lives a
thousand miles from the Atlantic Ocean, which is that I live a
thousand miles from the Atlantic Ocean and all fishing—like all
politics—is local.

I've always been charmed and intimidated by the mythology
of a fish that's not supposed to bite and, sure enough, usually
doesn't, but that can nonetheless sometimes be caught on flies
that look, to a trout guy at least, like accidents of fashion. I've
also always assumed that getting on good water took big money,
big connections, or both, while most of us have neither. In fact,
an old and somewhat disillusioned salmon fisher I met on the
Nepisiguit River more than ten years ago told me as much.
"If you have unlimited funds," he said, "you can catch all the
salmon you want." I remember doubting it was actually that
easy, but I understood what he was getting at.

The fly that worked that day was one Frenchy ties that
amounts to a small but significant variation of a traditional
Buck Bug. He refuses to name it or to call it his, although tiers

regularly claim lesser changes in existing patterns as their own. He's not secretive about the fly, and he'll show it to anyone and even give one away from time to time. He's not worried about the pattern being stolen or becoming too popular because, he said, "No one else can tie it right."

I learned a few useful things that day and with Frenchy's advice and flies I caught some fish, but there's an unbridgeable gap between the best fishermen and the rest of us. I've fished with several people who have written good books about how to catch this or that kind of game fish, and I can tell you that a full third of what they know—possibly the best third—isn't in the book because there's no way to put it there. What happens with the great ones is that after years of being attentive, something inside them relaxes and they finally begin to see what they've been looking at all along, but it's next to impossible to put that into a set of instructions that anyone can follow.

Toward the end of the day, we motored down to what Frenchy said was the first pool on the river: the first place where a salmon could rest after running out of the salt water. He said, matter of factly, "Any fish that's in here has never seen a fly before," and sure enough the big salmon I got there hit with a kind of heartbreaking innocence and hooked himself. I can't say I wasn't surprised when this silver slab went cartwheeling down the river evoking every salmon-fishing cliché I'd ever read, but all day I'd had the nagging sense that when you're fly casting from a fifty-year-old wooden canoe in the company of a Canadian named Frenchy, you're probably doing it right.

12

ROAD TRIP

The price of gas that summer (at historic highs through most of July) sucked some of the glamour out of a thousand-mile road trip, but not so much that it didn't still seem worth doing. So it wasn't the smartest time to climb into a gas-hog V-8 pickup and set off across the Rocky Mountains, but that was the only one of our vehicles that would hold all three of us, plus our camping and fishing gear, and that had four-wheel-drive to negotiate some of the roads we'd probably end up on. It's just that in these times—maybe in *all* times—living a good life takes a degree of dim-witted optimism, and some trips come with their own built-in moments that are too compelling to ignore or postpone. Ed Zern said, "The best time to go fishing is when you can." John Steinbeck said, "You don't take a trip; a trip takes you."

The idea came up in the organic way these things do. We were idly talking about cutthroats one day when Doug, who has a real jones for cutts, recalled a little creek in western Wyoming that he fished with a friend twenty-some years ago when they were both new to fly fishing. Some of the finer details had gone out of focus over time, but he clearly remembered the name and location of a pretty little stream with Snake River cutthroats up to twelve and fourteen inches long where, as a beginner, he actually got into fish for the first time as opposed to hooking one now and then almost by accident.

When Doug and his friend bragged about their day at a fly shop in the next town, the guy behind the counter shrugged it off, saying something like, "I guess that's okay if all you want is little fish." It's pointless to psychoanalyze your friends, but it occurred to me that this single incident could account for Doug's abiding love of cutthroats as well as his disdain for the suspiciously Freudian cult of size among some fly fishers.

That story reminded Vince of another stream in the same corner of Wyoming that he and Doug had fished ten years ago on a whim. They'd just picked up Vince's then-new drift boat in Idaho, and on the way back had stopped to kill a few hours wade-fishing a headwater stream. They didn't have a lot of time because they had to meet me in Saratoga for the boat's maiden voyage on the North Platte, but they caught so many nice trout that they had trouble pulling themselves away. Doug and I didn't know each other well then, and on the drive south he worried about being late, but Vince said, "We were catching fish; John will understand."

And then once a trip to the region was in the wind, a former guide, now boatbuilder, friend suggested another stream we should look at as long as we'd be in the area, and yet another friend—a former guide, now editor and filmmaker—added a few more names, and so on. (If you've ever wondered why so many of the best fishing guides eventually drift into other professions, just picture hard seasonal work, low pay, unreliable tips, and an unpredictable percentage of spoiled, demanding clients.) Anyway, each stream sounded tempting, and although the next one was always a little farther away than the last, no two were more than half a day's drive apart. This is how you get sucked into eating up the miles almost—but not quite—against your will.

In some ways, a trip like this is simply about the unambiguous accomplishment of getting from one place to another through a landscape that can be lush or desolate, but that in most of Wyoming is still blessedly empty. But then sometimes admitting your real motive is more trouble than it's worth. If a nonangler asks, "Why there?" the easy way out is to say "for the fishing," and he'll either understand or think he does. If you say something closer to the truth—that you just want to get your feet wet and sleep on the ground in some new, wild places—he'll look at you funny or, worse yet, conclude that you're a fellow New Age weenie and go all metaphysical on you. But then to any killjoy who says "That's an awful long way to drive for a few trout," you can honestly say, "That's the point."

The stream Doug and Vince had fished on the way back

from Idaho ten years ago was miles past the grizzly bear warn-
ing sign down a Forest Service road. We set up a quick camp
in the same copse of trees where they'd stashed the drift boat
a decade earlier and found the place to be infested with mosquitoes. Persistent swarms of them; the kind you'd normally
find in someplace like Labrador, where a guide once told me,
"If there were any more mosquitoes here, they'd have to be
smaller." Doug and Vince said they didn't remember the mosquitoes from the previous trip, but then they'd been there in
mid-September and this was July of a wetter year.

We fished that evening and all the next day, alternately
swatting mosquitoes and catching trout. There were caddis on
the water, two sizes of stonefly, assorted small mayflies, and
some of the size 12 Gray Drakes we'd been told to keep an eye
out for, sometimes singly, more often in some combination or
another. We got a few more strikes from small whitefish than
we'd have liked, but the trout we caught in between were fat
and healthy.

For two nights, we had one of those necessarily careful
camps. All you can do about mosquitoes is use bug dope, build
smudge fires to try to smoke them out, and avoid unzipping
your tent between eight in the morning and eight in the evening
so you can at least sleep bug-free. You can also take inordinate
satisfaction from squashing a single mosquito, even though it's
only one of millions. You think, I'll itch for a while and get better, but you're *dead*.

To avoid attracting bears, you try to cook without splattering
grease all over the place, wash the dishes thoroughly, and stash
food, utensils, and the clothes you wore when you cooked and
ate either in the truck or roped up a tree some distance from

camp. There's some debate about ritually peeing near the four corners of your tent. I favor temporarily staking out my little patch on the theory that it can't hurt and might help, but others claim that marking territory a bear might consider his could be seen as a challenge.

Beyond the usual precautions, you simply try to keep your imagination under control in order to avoid a nocturnal attack of the heebie-jeebies when any innocent night sound translates itself into a bloodthirsty eight-hundred-pound carnivore outside your tent. A friend told me that when he camps in bear territory, he always sleeps with earplugs. "If something happens that demands my attention, it'll be hard to miss," he said. "Otherwise, I don't wanna know about it."

One day we drove many miles on a bad dirt road that roughly paralleled a stream in the Gros Ventre Mountains. Our source—who used to guide in the area and fish this stream on his days off—had told us to get in above a certain point that turned out to be a godawful long, slow grind up this road. But then we've all learned that relative inaccessibility is usually a good thing in fishing and that if you're going to follow up on a tip at all, you should follow it to the letter.

The stream looked fine at first and it was hard not to stop and fish, but as we ground on up there, it began to go off-color until finally it was too opaque to fish and we stopped to study our map. We'd been in the area for several days and knew there had to be a point source for the mud because no rain had fallen. (What had looked like high clouds was actually the smoke from two wildfires: one down around Pinedale, the other up near Yellowstone.) I pointed at a spot on the map where, about a mile upstream, a tributary called Crystal Creek poured in, and said, "Before we give up, let's go see if that's coming in dirty."

So we drove up there to look and, sure enough, the creek was brown and thick enough to plow, but the main stream above the confluence was clear. Doug and Vince congratulated me on the call, but it was nothing. Any writer knows you can't go far wrong betting on the irony of Crystal Creek being muddy.

Where we finally got on it in midafternoon, the stream meandered down one of those high, wide valleys that are one-third willows and water and two-thirds blue sky. It was a fishy-looking stream, but at first we caught only a few small cut-throats, which was explained when we started seeing the fresh tracks of two fishermen and a large dog in odd patches of mud. We knew they were fishermen because the tracks were crisp and clear, but without tread marks—indicating felt soles—and they were in places where you wouldn't walk unless you were fishing. We kept seeing the tracks here and there for most of the next two miles, and then at precisely the spot where we lost them, we started catching some nice big cutthroats.

It was also somewhere in that third mile that I found part of an old buffalo skull sticking out of a cut bank—just a single horn with a ragged piece of bone attached. It was half rotted away and packed with dirt and roots, suggesting it had been buried in stream mud that became dry land when the channel shifted in a high runoff and then unearthed years later when the stream course moved back. (This was one of those restless western streams that wander around in their valleys from time to time as if they were looking for something.) The skull was obviously ancient, but there were still buffalo in the valley, and we decided a herd of these critters fording Crystal Creek could account for the mud. Of course, it could just as easily have been cows or even a bulldozer, but given the choice, who wouldn't settle on buffalo?

Two-thirds of the way through the trip, it was time for a town day: showers, laundry, a restaurant meal, and a bed with sheets, but not TV or newspapers. By definition, all road trips eventually end, which means you'll be checking back in with the shit storm soon enough.

These stops always involve a little culture shock. We'd been "Everywhere at once while going nowhere in particular," as Adam Gopnik once said of the way poets operate: following a meandering course in no particular hurry, camping and fishing small trout streams a drainage or two away from the main tourist routes. Many of those creeks were in places that are a testament to the effects of heat, cold, wind, and grit on the landscape as well as the inhabitants, who tend toward the hard-bitten, laconic side. Anyone who thinks that New York and L.A. set the tone for the rest of the country via television has never been to rural Wyoming.

Driving into a bustling tourist town past a sign saying WELCOME TO THE REAL WEST, you realize you're back on the grid and not really in the real West at all, but in a place that, as Ted Leeson said, has been "Bozemanized, Aspenated, or Jackson Holed out of existence." This was a summer of high gas prices and impending economic collapse, but there still seemed to be a lot of people traveling. There were the usual pods of recreational bikers driving motorcycles dripping with chrome and wearing Hell's Angels–inspired designer duds and headbands in lieu of helmets. Some of these guys managed to come off as convincingly threatening (although the few genuine tough guys

I've known didn't have to go out of their way to *look* tough), but
the reality is that you now have to be a corporate lawyer or brain
surgeon to afford a Harley, and your leathers alone can cost as
much as a custom-made three-piece suit.

For the record, I think motorcycles are beautiful machines
and I appreciate their iconography, but I can't stand the god-
damned noise.

On the other end of the scale are young families on a bud-
get: Mom, Dad, a couple of kids, and a dog shoehorned into a
minivan with enough stuff to stock a small sporting goods store.
This is the family vacation circa 1950 that I remember from my
own childhood, marked by boredom, discomfort, and short tem-
pers caused by whining, ungrateful kids. This trip is for them,
after all; so they can see some of the world in the flesh instead
of on TV. My own recollections include the hell on earth of con-
finement with the parents, the occasional desperate need to pee
with no relief in sight, and the kind of hokey roadside attrac-
tions that wouldn't fool a two-year-old. Those trips were pure
misery, but they somehow started me on a life of travel that I
wouldn't trade for anything.

Now and then the dad will glance at my friends and me—
three grown men traveling together in a muddy four-wheel-
drive pickup—with a look that's not so much envy as nostalgia.
Many men still view the minivan as a symbol of capitulation,
but this guy isn't the least bit sorry that he now has the family
and everything that goes with it; he just spends a minute or two
fondly remembering when he didn't.

There were even a few hitchhikers with backpacks around,
though fewer than there would have been thirty years ago.
They were mostly young, weathered, and slightly beat-up, but

in a strangely clean-cut sort of way. I remember hitchhiking as an awful way to travel unless you embraced the awfulness as a necessary element of the pilgrimage. You could stand for hours in the hot sun or pouring rain without getting a ride. You'd think rain would make drivers feel sorry for you—and maybe it did—but whatever pangs of conscience they had later, at the crucial moment of decision they usually passed on having a wet hippie in their car.

In my day, the legality of hitchhiking was usually unclear, but even if it wasn't actually illegal, it could still lead to a charge of vagrancy. In practice, it was often winked at unless the cops didn't like your looks—and they almost never liked your looks.

But for the moment, at least, all these kids wanted out of life was to be somewhere else under their own power. It didn't really matter where; they just needed to be strangers so they could begin to reinvent themselves away from the prying eyes of those who have known them since they were babies. A few of them may not yet have understood that, like me, they'll still be at it in their sixties, albeit a little less frantically and no longer on foot.

We ended up fishing a generous handful of small streams before we completed an uneven loop and started back. I guess it *did* amount to an awful long way to go for a few trout, but trips like this have nonetheless become a kind of part-time life's work. The idea is to fish obscure headwater creeks in hopes of eventually sniffing out an underappreciated little trout creek down an unmarked dirt road. "Why" is another question. I suppose it's partly for the fishing itself and partly to satisfy your curiosity, but mostly to sustain the belief that such things are still out there to find for those willing to look.

Of course, aimless travel is one of those things that no longer seem quite right for environmental reasons and the added bite on the bankroll for gas begins to look less like a temporary inconvenience and more like the real wages of sin. I'm still learning to be aware of the carbon footprint I leave in the world, as well as getting used to the idea that I even have one. I can clearly remember when if you asked someone about their carbon footprint, they'd have looked at their shoes to see if they'd stepped in something. On the other hand, being on the road for its own sake is still part of America's hyperventilated romance with itself, and lately when I travel like this, I remember dead friends, none of whose epitaphs read I WISH I'D WORKED HARDER AND FISHED LESS. Not to mention a live friend who recently said, "I assumed I'd be dead by the time the shit hit the fan, but no such luck."

We found Doug's little cutthroat creek easily enough—it was right there on the map where anyone could see it—and as we drove upstream, Doug said it looked familiar, with a long riffly stretch down low, steep white pocket water through a canyon, then a long bench higher up with wide bend pools.

We picked a likely-looking spot and fished for an hour or so. Nothing was said, but it was only late morning and I think we all understood there was still time to move on if it didn't pan out. Doug caught a single dink still in parr marks in a fishy-looking bend pool, then we leapfrogged up an apparently fishless riffle, and Vince and I caught nearly identical thirteen-inch Snake River cutts in a plunge pool. Doug said, "This is what I remember: not a lot of fish, but some nice ones," and without much more discussion we hiked back to the truck and went looking for a place to set up camp.

We avoid official campgrounds whenever possible because we don't like to pay and because in tourist season they remind us of middle-class refugee camps, although we've been known to pull into one to fill our water jugs from the communal spigot. So we drove around for a while and eventually found a near-perfect spot not far upstream. A little way off the main dirt road, an unmarked two-track dead-ended at a forested bench forty or fifty feet above the stream. It was high enough above the willow bottom to be away from mosquitoes, and the view took in a half mile of creek spread out to the south, the peaks of the Gros Ventres looming to the east, and a couple of snowcapped crags on the western horizon that would have had to be in the Tetons.

There were enough flat spots for the tents and the usual old rocked-in fire pit with some half-burned trash in it. The crusty dried ash in the bottom of the pit showed that the last ones there were smart enough to douse the fire with water before they left instead of leaving it to smolder dangerously—the most common and costly mistake made by inept campers. There were a few windfall lodgepole pines lying around with most of the wood that could be broken over a knee already used up, but we easily cut up the bigger branches with the small bow saw we carry—a useful piece of equipment most car campers wish they'd brought, but didn't.

Something else one of the campers who'd been there before us should have brought, but apparently didn't, is a small folding shovel sometimes called an entrenching tool. This is used to bury the remains when you relieve yourself, which is preferable in every way to leaving exposed turds and the scraps of toilet paper guides call "white flags." For more information, consult the modern Bible on this important subject, *How to Shit in the Woods: An Environmentally Sound Approach to a Lost Art*, by Kathleen Meyer.

Two days later, we'd just come up from the creek after an evening rise, had a fire going, and were getting ready to cook some elk tenderloins I'd brought frozen from home. We'd spent the better part of both days catching more wild Snake River cutts than any of us expected—including Doug with his old but fond memories—and that afternoon I'd landed a nineteen-inch slab of a cutthroat that was the kind of fish we small-stream guys say we're willing to forgo in favor of scenery and solitude. Doug took a photo of the fish held next to the rod I was using, and I've since sent a print to the rod maker. This is a strategy that allows you to openly brag about a big fish while seeming to be doing a favor for someone else.

The fire was just about down to good grilling coals when an older couple pulled in at the end of the two-track fifty yards to the west. The man stayed with the car and started rigging up two fly rods, while the woman walked over to say that they'd had their first fly-fishing lesson that day and would we mind if they fished here. I wondered if they'd been taught some stream etiquette in their fly-fishing lesson (one can only hope) or if they were just instinctively polite. I said of course we didn't mind, but that we'd just gotten off the water and had probably spooked the fish. She said that was okay, they probably wouldn't know the difference, the kind of self-deprecating remark you often hear from beginners.

As we cooked and ate dinner on our vantage point above the stream, we watched these two fish and agreed that for people who'd had their first fly-fishing lesson that day, they were doing surprisingly well, though probably not quite well enough to actually catch a trout.

It occurred to me only later that we should have gone down there and offered a little help. There'd have been no guarantees, but Doug and I are experienced fly fishers and Vince is a casting instructor, so at the very least we probably wouldn't have done any harm. I'm sorry now that we didn't because among the joys of traveling are those small kindnesses between strangers, whichever side of them you happen to be on. This isn't the kind of thing that will keep me awake at night; it's just one of those small regrets you bring home from any trip.

13

CHEATING

In the introduction to his 1978 anthology, *Silent Seasons*, Russell Chatham politely said of fishing, "It's possible too many judgments have been passed regarding the purity or merit of one type over another." Twenty-five years later, in a novel called *The Summer Guest*, Justin Cronin put a finer point on it when he said, "The fact is, there's a great deal of hairsplitting fussiness when it comes to fly-fishing, most of it as silly as a top hat." Which is to say, not much has changed in a quarter century.

It was in the 1970s that I was first learning what became known as short-line nymphing, which is the same thing they call Czech nymphing now. At the time, it was considered to be the hot new method on the South Platte River in Colorado, although I've since traced it as far back as the 1930s when a private club on the same river threatened to kick out a member if he didn't stop cheating by fishing nymphs ahead of split shot. The problem, they said, was that he was catching too many trout.

But that was just the first written record I could find from my home state. The method is actually as old as the hills and was adapted from earlier generations of practical types who used fly rods to fish artificial flies, live grasshoppers, worms, salmon eggs, and grubs indiscriminately, with or without sinkers. According to some of the old meat fishers I've talked to, they used flies when they had to, but flies cost money, while you could dig your own bait for free. They fished long fly rods—usually nine-footers—for their extra reach while bait fishing as well as for their ability to cast flies. These guys were out to catch fish, and style was not a big consideration.

Anyway, as late as the 1970s, nymphing with added weight on the leader was still considered by the fly-fishing intelligentsia to be cheating, or at least so said the editor of a fishing magazine when I tried to sell him an article about it.

At the time, fly fishing in America was still a deeply traditional sport with a strong British influence and a large population of dry-fly purists, but it was beginning to be infiltrated by young, counterculture types. These new people liked the old-timey artfulness of fly-fishing, but were less bound by custom than some of the older guys. Their lifestyles were also a little different, which could lead to some awkward misunderstandings. I remember hanging out in a slightly tweedy fly shop one afternoon where the owner was promoting the first generation of powdered desiccant used as a fly floatant. A young hippie friend of mine walked in—complete with long hair and a tie-dyed T-shirt—and the owner asked, "Have you been using the magic powder?" The guy said, "Yeah, man, but not when I'm fishing."

So there was more room for new ideas than there'd been before, but that young generation of fly fishers didn't change the sport as drastically as you might think. Contrary to what they say now, we didn't reject everything, we simply reserved the right to decide what we'd accept as is, what we'd ignore, and what we'd reinvent. So some of these young guys were gonzo innovators willing to try anything, while others became old-school dry-fly purists fishing with the second- and third-tier Golden Age bamboo rods that hadn't yet been discovered by collectors, so we could still afford them. Many of us had taken up fly fishing not so much as a sport, but as a possible path to enlightenment, and as everyone knows, those routes aren't the same for everyone and they're never clearly marked. You just head out in whatever seems like the right direction at the time.

A precious few of these guys got pretty far off the grid. There was a legendary character around here back then known as Snowshoe John who was said to live in a series of semipermanent camps in the national forest where he hunted, trapped, snared, gathered, and fished for his food—presumably without the benefit of licenses or much regard for the seasons. We knew about him because some who reported sightings of the guy said that the butt of a fly rod with a Hardy reel attached could be seen sticking out of his backpack. He was seen as a visionary back-to-nature type at first, but as time went by, he got progressively stranger until—before he finally disappeared alto-gether—he became a spooky mound of hair in a greasy parka who was now and then seen hitchhiking on mountain roads: a certified wild man and not the guy you'd pick to have a thought-ful discussion about the ethics of fly fishing.

As for nymphing with weight, it was controversial for a while and then it wasn't, complete with footnotes. Even after it was more or less accepted, there were those who said the method itself was okay, but you were cheating if you used a strike indi-cator. Others said a strike indicator was permissible as long as it was used to actually indicate strikes, but it was cheating if you used it as a bobber to suspend the flies. Some claimed you should use only a single nymph, while others said there was nothing wrong with fishing a brace or even a gang of flies. It was a period of what you might call hairsplitting fussiness.

The only convincing criticism I ever heard of nymphing was Lee Wulff's dictum that "trout deserve the sanctuary of deep water." Pissing matches over who's better than whom and why are usually pretty boring, but arguments that come from respect for the game always seem compelling. This was the time when catch-and-release fishing was beginning to catch on as a management tool, and a light touch instead of a heavy hand did seem better from a conservation standpoint. You also couldn't deny that there was a kind of poetry to waiting all day for a hatch so you can spend an hour catching them on dry flies, although that took more patience than most of us could mus-ter. Still, I know a guide who now regularly has his clients use nymphs in order to catch fish but makes them switch to dries when the trout start to rise. If they ask why, he says, "Because that's how it's done."

It seems to me that most of the new developments in tackle and tactics in the last thirty years or so were seen as cheating for a while before they were first grudgingly accepted and then finally became standard practice. Before the advent of commercial sink-tip lines, we used to get the same effect by splicing various lengths of lead-core trolling line between our floating fly lines and leaders using loop-to-loop connections. These rigs were awful to cast and nowhere near as elegant as the customized shooting heads the West Coast steelheaders were building at the time, but they sure did get a streamer down deep. Younger fly fishers like I was at the time usually thought this was a pretty cool idea, while an older fly caster was more likely to say, "Well, hell, why don't you just go ahead and use bait?"

For as long as I can remember, that's been the worst thing you could say to a fly fisher: that whatever he was doing might as well be bait fishing. Supposedly, bait fishing is too easy, while the whole idea of sport has to do with self-imposed limitations that level the field. (If you armed one team in a football game with chain saws, they'd score more touchdowns, guaranteed, but it would be too one-sided to hold your interest for long.)

I first heard that argument from my father in the 1950s. He said that fishing any kind of artificial lure was superior to bait because you had to convince the fish the thing was something it wasn't, while with bait the fish wasn't actually fooled. As Dad said, "He thinks it's a worm and it really *is* a worm. Where's the skill in that?" Of course, it was hard for me to think of bait as being too easy because some of my earliest fishing involved staring for hours at a bobber that refused to move: not your average seven-year-old's idea of nonstop action. (At least when you were trolling, the scenery changed, albeit slowly.) And anyway, if bait was so damned easy, why wasn't I getting more fish?

But then I was just an innocent kid, still unaware of the layers of nit-picking that had settled on the sport. I only learned later that some fly fishers look down their noses at bait and lure fishermen as low-rent and unskilled, while the worm and gear guys who care one way or another tend to view fly fishers as conceited dilettantes. That's one argument I try not to get involved in. With the environment generally going from bad to worse, I've always thought we should all band together to save the remaining fisheries and rehabilitate others where possible. Once that's done, we can go ahead and fight over how the fish should be caught.

Fishing snobbery isn't pretty, but I've been around it for a long time and, truth be known, have even engaged in it a time or two, so I understand the psychology. Life is an unruly mess and ideals are hard to hold on to, but fishing is an isolated enough slice of it that there's the hope we can do this one small thing perfectly. But then perfection is a matter of aesthetics, so that what's right is just what *feels* right, which is naturally different for everyone who picks up a rod. At its worst, snobbery is a vain attempt by the insecure to elevate themselves by denigrating others as cheaters, but at its best, it's an honest attempt to do a beautiful thing as well as it can possibly be done.

I've always had a soft spot for dry flies because I think they're just the prettiest way to catch trout and because elevating dry-fly fishing to a moral imperative, as some of the chalk stream fishermen in England did in the 1800s, now seems irresistibly quaint. I even flirted with being a purist myself for a while, but never could get past my midwestern Germanic practicality. When I was first learning to fly-fish, a friend and I used to meet after work on a local trout stream where we'd fish bait with our fly rods until we each had a brace of trout for dinner. Then we'd switch to flies and try to catch and release a few more before dark. It was a great moment when we finally started depending on proper dry flies for the groceries, but I can't say the trout tasted any better.

So I have my preferences, but I'm also less interested in being right than I once was and now think any kind of fishing done well is an art. That would include casting throw nets and baited hand lines in the Sea of Cortez and spearing pike through the ice in Minnesota. The one sure path to humiliation is to try a new kind of fishing after saying there can't be much to it.

Still, one fly fisher will say that trout are obviously superior to bass because they're prettier and harder to catch, while a bass guy will say he thinks largemouths are more tastefully handsome than trout and plenty hard to catch in their own right. Another fisherman will say steelhead are better than both because they're bigger, while a fourth might say that a fixation on size indicates penis envy. I've actually heard all that said, just not at the same time and place, and it's occurred to me that non-anglers who tend to see fishermen as harmlessly goofy and picturesque would be amazed to learn how unforgiving we can be among ourselves

There's even a lingering prejudice among some against the fly pattern known as the San Juan Worm. It fits the most politically correct criteria of being an almost perfect copy of a common aquatic organism, but it's too easy to tie and the word "worm" in the fly's name keeps some fishermen from using it because the dark implication of bait is too onerous.

If you're looking for logic here, don't bother. Minnows are

also commonly used as bait, but I've yet to see someone turn up his nose at a Muddler Minnow streamer because of its name.

What the proper way to fish might be can make for interesting philosophical discussions, but as ironclad snootiness—complete with accusations of cheating against those who don't strictly adhere to doctrine—it seems pointless. If we wanted to be completely blameless in terms of conservation, we'd fish without hooks. If all we wanted was a body count, we'd use dynamite. Meanwhile, one fisherman says nymph fishing is bad because it's too efficient, while the next says it's good precisely *because* it's efficient. I'm told that in 1953, when Al McClane published a book called *The Practical Fly Fisherman,* some rushed to buy it, while others shrugged and said, "There's nothing practical about fly-fishing. That's the whole point."

And then just when you think you have it figured out—for yourself if not for everyone else—something new comes along. On a trip to Alaska a few years ago, I discovered flap-doodles. These are small orange or hot-pink spinner blades attached to a fly at the bend of the hook with a small barrel swivel. They're used by guides to get their clients into fish when the king salmon aren't biting as they could be and they work almost too well. One inquisitive guide discovered they're so effective that a bare hook with the flap-doodle attached worked better than any fly pattern, although the lodge manager asked him to keep that quiet.

Some fly fishers use flap-doodles without batting an eye on the premise that you should always fish as the locals do; others simply refuse to fish hardware on a fly rod under any circumstances; and still others are leery at first, but then quickly tumble when they see their partners catching fish while they're not. And that about sums up the entire controversy.

It's tempting to say we all at least agree that poaching is cheating, but it's interesting that although we can get into a positive snit about fine points of tackle and execution, out-and-out poaching still has an aura of outlaw romance in the minds of many otherwise law-abiding fishermen. I got my first clear view of this nearly fifty years ago from an uncle who told me, as we were quietly sneaking through a barbed-wire fence, that fish belong only to God and the People.

I can't honestly say I've never broken a fishing law, but I *can* say it didn't happen often even when I was a reckless boy, and it was so long ago it seems like the crimes were committed by someone I once knew and now barely remember. I can also say it's much easier to want to do things right once you've done them wrong a few times to see how it feels. If nothing else, it's hard to concentrate while looking over your shoulder.

This isn't just an American phenomenon. When I was salmon fishing in Scotland years ago, there was grudging respect for a local poacher who regularly trespassed on private estates and killed salmon that didn't belong to him because he insisted on catching them with a fly rod and a proper single-hook salmon fly. The guy was widely considered to be a bounder and a thief by wealthy landowners, but as a fly fisherman, his credentials were impeccable, and among some locals he was a regional hero.

According to the story, his justification was that these were actually his fish because the Duke of Cumberland had taken the salmon rivers from the native highlanders in 1746 at an event known to the winners as the Battle of Culloden and to the losers as the Culloden Massacre. Even if that was just a convenient excuse, it still illustrates the lesson about wars that we never seem to learn: namely, that they never quite end.

The mythology of the amateur poacher says he does it out of some hard-bitten subsistence motive, although in my limited experience, they do it for sport and few of them are actually trying to feed children who'd otherwise go hungry. Still, the unspoken ethical code says that although you've crossed the line between sport and crime, you should still take only what you need and deserve. The first part is easy enough to determine, but that second part can be a head-scratcher.

In fact, most poachers don't really think they're above the law, just that they're off to the side of it in some fun-loving, anarchistic way. There are countless references to this attitude in American folklore, including a verse in Woody Guthrie's populist anthem "This Land Is Your Land" where Guthrie sees a sign that says no trespassing on one side, "But on the other side/It didn't say nothin'/That side was made for you and me."

Speaking of signs, a well-known local poacher once told me that he'd hiked the long way around to a private lake carrying a belly boat, but when he got there, he discovered he'd forgotten his flippers. So using a pair of pliers and the roll of duct tape he always carries, he fashioned a pair of flippers using two aluminum NO TRESPASSING signs he pried off of nearby trees. When I made a skeptical face, he showed me the flippers. He still had them behind the seat in his pickup.

Another poaching story comes from just over the state line in Wyoming. There was a guy who regularly poached a local ranch with a privately leased trout stream on it. He'd come in overland at night, often on horseback, quietly fill a gunny sack with stolen trout, and then vanish into the surrounding foothills. In one version of the story, he'd fished the stream all his life, boy and man, and was rankled at the idea that wealthy fishermen could pull his birthright out from under him simply by writing a check. Then again, it's possible this detail was added to the story later to make the guy seem more like a righteous desperado and less like a petty crook. Anyway, he bragged about his exploits, so his identity was commonly known in the small ranching community, although of course there was no proof.

When he was finally caught red-handed, he was hauled into court, convicted, fined, and prohibited from buying a fishing license for a couple of years—not that a poacher would care much about that. On the way out of the courtroom, he ran into the rancher who'd pressed charges and who'd come to watch the proceedings. The two men shook hands amiably; they were neighbors, after all.

The poacher said, "See you next year, Bob."

The rancher smiled and replied, "We'll keep an eye out for you."

14

FIREWOOD

I was walking up a stream near home wearing hip boots and carrying a fly rod when I ran into a hiker who asked, "Are there fish in here?" To be polite and because I guess it was an innocent enough question, I said, "Yes, there are some small trout," but it seemed like an odd thing to ask a guy who's obviously fishing. On the other hand, maybe I had the all-too-common look of someone who didn't know what the hell he was doing. You see that a lot these days.

A little farther on a guy walking his Australian shepherd asked a more astute question: "Are you catching any or just getting out for the afternoon?" As it turned out, I *was* just getting out, but I hadn't even strung up the rod yet, so I said it was early and things could still go either way. He nodded in an understanding way that made me think this was a guy who either fished himself or at least had a family history of the condition.

I like everything about fishing, but especially this walk in before you've even tied on a fly. You never know what to expect—and in the winter you don't expect much—but the goal of going fishing has already been accomplished, so the rest is the aimless, doglike happiness of being outside and off your leash.

People were out and talkative that day because this was the first stretch of decent weather we'd had in seven weeks. It was early February, and it had been sunny with daytime highs briefly into the low 50s for several days in a row, while for part of December and all of January, temperatures hadn't risen above freezing. At one point after the second of two major blizzards, my neighbor measured the snow covering his meadow at forty-two inches deep.

Snow is always welcome here in Colorado, but too much at once can be awful if you're a rancher with stranded and starving cattle or if you've set up a permanent camp on the floor at Denver International Airport. But then I'm self-employed, a little reclusive, and had nowhere in particular to go, so I enjoyed it. I also enjoyed telling complainers that when I was a kid in Minnesota we used to go to the beach in weather like this. The only drawback was that I was running low on firewood. Most years I can get through a winter on three cords. This year I'd gone through five and had started on a sixth.

In fact, that's why I was up at the stream in the first place. Off and on since the previous fall, the powers that be had been thinning the overgrown ponderosa pine forest in the area for fire protection, and since this is public land, they'd been hauling the logs out and dumping them along the road for anyone to take. There were no announcements and nothing resembling a schedule, just the word of mouth that at various unpredictable times there'd be large piles of free firewood lying by the side of the road. You just had to drive up there now and then to check.

Of course, this stuff would often come out as logs too long and heavy to handle, so when you *did* go up to check, you had to bring along a saw, gas, bar and chain oil, and all the niggling little wrenches, screwdrivers, and files it takes to keep an aging chainsaw sharp and running. There was no coming back later at your convenience. It was the tail end of a long, cold winter, firewood was at a premium, and people had gotten on to this.

But then since you're going to a trout stream anyway and since there may or may not be any cutting and hauling to do, you might as well throw in a fly rod and all the niggling doodads it takes to make *that* tool work. It's only a ten-minute drive, but why waste a trip?

This little stream isn't especially rich and the trout aren't all that big or numerous, but it lies between two foothill reservoirs, and the one at the upstream end has a bottom-draw dam that produces just enough of a tailwater effect to keep it open and at least theoretically fishable through the winter. The two-mile access road up to the dam is gated, but they keep it plowed, so even in deep snow you can walk along the stream without resorting to snowshoes. It's known locally as nothing to write home about, but like all streams that you'll hear described as

141

mediocre, it can reward the fly fisher who has reasonable expectations and who gives it the time and effort it deserves.

So anyway, I drove up to the stream and there was no wood, but there *were* six or seven cars parked at the gate. I couldn't identify any of them as being owned by fishermen I knew, so I went through the usual drill. First, I looked for TROUT UNLIMITED decals or A BAD DAY OF FISHING IS BETTER THAN A GOOD DAY AT WORK bumper stickers and didn't see any. Then I moseyed around casually glancing in car windows, trying not to look too suspicious as I scanned for rod cases or wader bags. But most of the SUVs had tinted windows, so I couldn't see in. Local fishermen do know about this spot, but it's also popular with hikers, so there was a chance these were all young couples walking their labradoodles.

I hiked up the stream, and when I topped the first rise, I could see that the lower reservoir was frozen and that kids testing the veracity of the DANGER ICE UNSAFE sign had lobbed out a fresh batch of cantaloupe-sized rocks. But then the inlet to the reservoir was open and so was the stream above, as it almost always is. I walked on up to a pair of adjacent pools about a mile and half upstream that, for reasons I've never figured out, are more likely to produce a winter midge hatch than anywhere else on this whole stretch. I didn't see any other fishermen, although I did talk to a few people and the dogs that were willing to say hello. Most people rightly assume that fishermen are completely approachable, while some dogs are understandably suspicious of a strange man wearing rubber pants and carrying a long stick.

As it turned out, there were five or six small brown trout rising quietly in the lower of the two pools, loosely podded up on the far side of the slow main current. They were feeding on the tiniest pale midge flies imaginable: roughly the size and color of wheat chaff and not much more than beige specks on the water.

The short version is that I put in a careful half hour of casting and couldn't get a strike, even with the smallest flies and the lightest tippet I had. I never actually spooked the trout and even got a couple of half-interested looks, but eventually, one by one, they figured out something wasn't right and quietly went away. I could see the fish distinctly in the low, clear water, and the biggest of them might have gone nine or ten inches.

On the hike out, I ran into my friend Todd Hosman and we stopped to compare notes. He was on his way to the pools I'd just come from and didn't seem all that disappointed to learn that I'd already fished them, especially when I said I'd gotten skunked and showed him the sparsely tied size 24 flies I'd been fishing on 7x tippet. He said he did okay up there the day before yesterday and showed me the size 32 emergers he'd been fishing on 8x.

When I took the box from him to look at the flies, Todd laughed and said he'd shown them to a mutual friend the other day who'd gotten the same disgusted scowl on his face.

I said, "I'm not scowling, I'm just trying to focus."

I also briefly wondered how much trouble a guy should go to in order to catch a few little trout, but then any fish becomes worth catching to the extent that you can't catch it, so the answer was obvious: Once you decide to try, you go to as much trouble as it takes.

I might have left it at that except for the firewood. It was free, I needed it, and it was next to impossible to buy any. All the commercial cutters I knew were telling the same story. They had plenty of wood on the ground, but the snow had kept them from getting it out, and once they *did* get it out, it would still need to be unloaded, bucked, split, reloaded, and delivered, starting with the long-standing back orders. The upshot was, it could take the better part of a month to get a cord of wood even if the thaw held, which it wouldn't.

But then on the way out that day, I ran into the local ranger putting along on his ATV. (His name is Dennis, but everyone calls him "Ranger Rick.") He knew I'd scarfed up a bunch of this wood the previous fall, so he told me that with the snow clearing off they'd be bringing out what he described as "shit-loads" of wood over the next week or so.

A few days later, I was back up at the creek with a freshly oiled and sharpened chainsaw, plus a spool of 8x tippet and half a dozen size 28 dry flies. Instead of tying on actual size 32 hooks, I'd used an old trick from the days before hooks that small became available. That is, I tied what amounted to size 32 flies on the forward half of size 28 hook shanks in what a salmon tier would call a "low water" style. I hadn't tied flies that small in quite a few years, but I found it was still no harder for me than separating paper coffee filters, which is difficult but not impossible. It's mostly a matter of attitude. My old friend and fly guru A. K. Best once told me that tying a size 28 fly was just like tying a size 16, except it was smaller. That didn't turn out to be precisely true, but it *was* instructive in a metaphorical sort of way.

In the simplest terms of being able to catch fish you couldn't catch before, I think the advent of tiny fly-tying hooks and the extrafine tippets you need to fish them is the single most important development in fly tackle in my lifetime, with no exceptions. Once the hooks became widely available, small flies naturally became a specialty for some, but remained a curiosity for others. (To this day, few commercial tiers tie flies smaller than a size 22, because they don't sell.) There's also been some legitimate controversy over extremely small flies. In the 1970s, about the time Arnold Gingrich, the founder of *Esquire* magazine, introduced the idea of the 20/20 club—where the goal was to hook and land a twenty-inch trout on what was then considered to be a near-microscopic-sized 20 fly—British fishing writers Brian Clarke and John Goddard described the American penchant for catching fish on tackle too light to adequately land them as an "unsporting affectation."

It's true that in most situations you can land a ten-inch trout with authority on a size 28 fly and 8x tippet (assuming you can hook it in the first place) but not so much as the fish get bigger, and it does finally become a pointless exercise to release an eighteen- or twenty-inch trout that you've already played to death. Like most of the fly fishers I know, I'd think about this whenever it came up, although for the most part, I usually just fell back on the old admonition that you should either land 'em or lose 'em, but don't screw around with 'em. After all, when you're fishing the smallest possible flies on the lightest available tippets, you're on the kind of extreme edge where you can't reasonably expect a high success rate.

As it turned out, there was the promised shitload of wood dumped by the road that day, and I cut and loaded as much as my pickup would hold without bottoming out the shocks— which is about two-thirds of a cord. Then I put a rod together and walked up to the pools. Either there wasn't much of a hatch that day or I'd come in right at the end of it. Whichever it was, there were only a few scattered rises on the lower pool, but I did manage to get one strike, which I missed.

Of course, the smaller the hook you use, the harder it is to hook and hold a fish, but when things get this delicate, even a buggered strike is a victory. If nothing else, it tells you your fly was small enough and at least that one cast and drift were adequate.

So this became the almost daily routine for the next week and a half. I didn't always find a fresh load of wood and rising trout on the same day, but as luck would have it, I always found one or the other.

I also usually found Todd. He'd gotten pretty interested in this hatch, too, if only because there wasn't much else happening close to home in February. Some days he'd get there first and beat me to the pools. Other days I'd beat him. One day I passed him quietly as he was fishing a pool lower down on the stream. (Someone watching might have assumed that I snuck by behind him in order to get to the pools upstream first, but the story I'm sticking to is that he seemed deeply involved and I didn't want to bother him.) Yet another day we ran into each other at the access road gate, hiked up to the pools together and shared the water. On the walk in, I mentioned that I liked the bottom pool best. He said he preferred the top one and so that's how we split them up. If he was being gracious—as I suspect he was—it was a pretty smooth maneuver.

By the time the weather turned cold and it started to snow again, I'd put in five cords of firewood and had caught a handful of trout. (On my best afternoon, I hooked five and landed three.) Most of my lost fish just came off, but the one big one—maybe fourteen inches—bent open the size 28 hook when I put the wood to him to try to keep him out of a sweeper.

Fine tippet is much stronger than it used to be. Not that long ago, the best 7x you could get had a breaking strength of eight ounces; today 8x tests out at around a pound and a half. But the metallurgy of hook making hasn't entirely caught up, so where you once would have broken off the fly, you now bend open the hook—with the same result that the big fish gets away. This is what we call "progress."

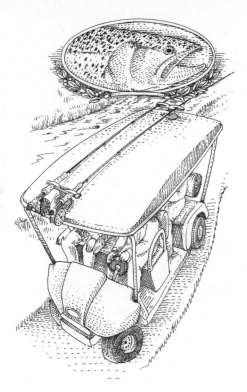

15

THE OTHER HALF

A landowner on Colorado's West Slope once asked my friend
A. K. Best and me if we'd stop by and "evaluate his fishery" for
him. We agreed because this was an odd, but not outrageous,
request and because it was also flattering, at least by implication. I mean, you wouldn't ask just anyone off the street, right?

We didn't learn until we arrived that this was a real estate
deal. The guy had bought a ranch and had built a pair of good-
sized lakes and some smaller ponds using water rights from

a stream that ran through the property. The next step was to develop the place into multimillion-dollar home sites with an extra million or so tacked on to the price for what he called "the trophy fishing." If we'd known the setup beforehand, we'd have tried to charge a consulting fee, but by then we were already there and he was putting us up in a cabin built to house prospective buyers, so what the hell.

The lakes had just lately been dug—probably that spring so they could be filled by the runoff—and they still had the raw, scraped look of a construction site. The water was clear, but the banks and the bottom were both just bare dirt with no vegetation beyond some scattered knapweed sprouting in the scarified soil. There were trout, though: pale hatchery rainbows between twenty-two and twenty-eight inches long, some with tails rubbed raw against the concrete raceways where they'd spent their lives until recently. There was no sign of aquatic insects or any other natural food organisms. The fish were easy to catch because they were starving.

We spent a mildly amusing day alternately catching big trout that fought lackadaisically and fending off a sense of sheepishness as the phrase "shooting fish in a barrel" kept coming to mind. Then the guy took us out to dinner and after some small talk asked, "So, what do you think?" There was an uncomfortable silence during which I remembered my grandmother telling me, "If you can't say something nice, don't say anything at all." Finally, A.K. cleared his throat and said, "Well, it *is* a little contrived, isn't it?"

Ten years later, I inadvertently found myself back at the same place, marveling at how life, which we like to think of as linear, actually progresses in a series of weirdly interlocking circles. The owner of a bookstore in the nearby town had asked me if I'd come up and do a book signing. To make the trip worthwhile, he said, he'd arrange to have me and a friend put up in a nice place and get us into a few days of good local fishing. (I've learned not to disabuse anyone who thinks they have to sweeten the pot to get me to promote my own book.) I asked my friend Doug if he wanted to go, and of course he did. That corner of the state is known for some good fishing and any red-blooded fly caster will jump at a tip on new water.

It turned out that the developer and the bookstore guy were friends and the "nice place" was the same cabin A.K. and I had stayed in a decade earlier. I should have seen that coming but didn't. Of course, the project was long since finished and sold out by then. The roads were paved and the ranch was now behind a forbidding iron gate that opened automatically when you punched a code into a keypad. But the cabin was just as I remembered it: comfortable and aggressively rustic in a sterile sort of way, with a marble powder room as big as a hotel lobby—an interior decorator's idea of a fishing shack.

The lakes had softened over the last decade. You still wouldn't mistake them for natural bodies of water, but there were now beds of aquatic weeds and a fringe of cattails and reeds around the shore, although the effect was mitigated by forty yards of manicured lawn between the cabin and the water. Platforms made of Volkswagen-sized rocks had been slid into the water at strategic points, so you could cast without getting your shoes wet unless the automatic sprinkler system happened to come on. The only thing that seemed unintentional was the extended family of meadow voles living under the cabin.

The trout in the lakes were also a little more realistic. The average rainbow was now between sixteen and eighteen inches long (a size that's cheaper to stock) with some larger holdovers twenty inches and better. Most of the trout would happily eat the standard slowly retrieved black Woolly Bugger, but some of the bigger ones had been caught and released enough to have become suspicious and needed extra convincing. They were still a little contrived as trout lakes go, but in the heat of casting to fish that wouldn't always bite, it was possible to forget that for minutes at a time.

Still, there's a vague sense of the feedlot to some stocked ponds: the idea of animals born, raised, fattened, and delivered for human consumption. On the other hand, a stocked trout in a pond probably lives a more authentic life than a steer preparing for the last roundup at Burger King. If nothing else, a trout could fight hard and get away or refuse to bite in the first place, while few steers escape their ultimate fate as hamburger.

In fact, some of the private stocked waters I've fished came complete with legends of just such monster holdover trout. These would be old hatchery fish that wised up early, turned feral in every way that counts, and are now sometimes seen as huge, gliding shadows, but are never caught. Guesses at their probable age vary, but on average they've grown to around ten pounds in the members' collective imagination. Considering the normal fisherman's propensity for hysteria, you could rightfully wonder if some of these fish even exist, but I know of one that was finally found dead of old age one early summer morning. The body measured just a hair less than thirty inches long. An informal necropsy revealed that its last meal had consisted of a baby muskrat. Maybe that's why this behemoth was never taken on a size 12 damsel fly nymph.

Another ranch we fished on that trip had a mile or so of river flowing through it in addition to the usual stocked ponds. Of course, the river had been stocked, too, but thankfully it hadn't been "improved" in any way. Once you were down along the water, the river seemed undisturbed and most of the expensive summer homes weren't visible behind the cottonwoods and willows. By then Doug and I had realized that there'd been a slight misunderstanding. When the bookstore owner said he'd arranged for us to fish on a couple of local ranches, we pictured muddy two-track roads, rusty barbed wire, ranch hands in greasy Stetsons, and actual cattle. We'd forgotten that the term "ranch" can have a different meaning in the New West.

To specify what we had in mind, you now have to say "*working* ranch," and that's what most of these places once were and would be still if not for the usual economic mud bath. Raising beef has always been a tough job. There's only one way it can go right and hundreds of ways for it to go wrong. In many cases, the ranchers who sold these places were tired and land-poor, and the final coffin nail was rising property taxes driven by the upscale development in the area. But even before that, they'd have been breaking even at best, or more likely losing money. (The joke has always been, "The way to make a million dollars ranching is to start with *two* million.") Their kids either didn't want to inherit the place—preferring to move to town, sleep late, and make an actual living—or would have liked to live the old life but saw they couldn't make a go of it any more than the old man had.

When the owner finally caved to a developer, his neighbors would have envied him for getting out clean in the end, even if they privately thought he'd violated a cultural trust. The developers themselves like to say these old ranchers retire comfortably to Florida, but that's doubtful. In the usual scenario, they move to a small bungalow in the nearest town and spend their sunset years hanging out with cronies at the feed store, shaking their heads at the way things turned out.

We checked in at the main ranch office to meet our guide, as instructed. He was a pleasant guy in his mid-twenties named Will, and it turned out I knew his Aunt Wendy, who guides for smallmouth bass in Wisconsin. (Small world; it must run in the family, etc.) When Doug and I said we could probably get along without a guide, Will politely insisted that he come with us. I don't know if that was ranch policy, but I do know there's a rare breed of angler who wouldn't fish without a guide any more than he'd golf without a caddy. Will also insisted that we ride to the river in the golf cart fitted with rod racks that he picked us up in, even though we were within sight of the water. Doug turned to me and whispered, "It's okay; no one we know will see us."

Later, I asked Doug how it was that a perfectly normal blue-collar fishing guide didn't seem the least bit embarrassed by the golf cart. Doug, who understands these things, said, "It's his job not to be embarrassed."

It couldn't have been better weather for fishing that week. We were in a mountain basin at around 7,000 feet in mid-August, where you'd expect bright sun, cumulus clouds in a blue sky, highs near 80, and the usual warm afternoon breeze. There'd be the usual late-summer thunderstorms, but they'd come and go quickly and wouldn't usually hurt the fishing. But the past few days had been unrelentingly gray, chilly, and wet, with rain squalls lower down and snow just a few hundred feet higher up. This was the kind of wintry late-summer storm we sometimes get in the Colorado mountains, though not quite often enough to get used to.

A few days earlier, we'd planned to drive over to the West Slope over Fall River Pass on Trail Ridge Road. That scenic route adds a good hour to the trip, but it's worth it for the view from the highest paved road in North America. But the pass was closed because of eight inches of fresh snow, so we had to cut south and take the interstate instead.

We learned later that we were only on the fitful backside of an upslope storm that had nestled against the Front Range hours after we left. It continued to snow in the national park and rained hard for the entire three days of the annual outdoor folk festival in the town of Lyons near where we both live. The streams got high and muddy and the streets ran with water, but the show went on and the wet festivarians cheerfully renamed the event the Soak Festival.

Susan, the woman I've lived with for the last fifteen years, claims that every time I go fishing for any length of time, some catastrophe happens back home that has to be either endured or dealt with; anything from an act of God to a plugged-up toilet. "How do you manage that?" she sometimes asks. Just lucky, I guess.

Anyway, it was unseasonably wet and chilly for August, with good summer stream flows, the usual late-summer crop of grasshoppers, and the kind of damp, gray autumnal weather that makes trout hungry and aggressive. We fished the grasshopper patterns Will suggested and caught pretty rainbow-cutthroat hybrids between sixteen and nineteen inches long, plus a few brown trout. We also pounded a deeply undercut bank where there was supposed to be an enormous brown that Will said had been seen a few times and even hooked once or twice but never landed. It wasn't home, wasn't interested, or didn't exist.

I was happy to see something besides the usual hatchery rainbows. Rainbow trout are fine fish in their own right and the wild ones are magnificent, but they're raised in such numbers and stocked so widely in both public and private water that they've become ubiquitous and generic. It's hard not to have mixed feelings about a trout that's so easily domesticated, and I guess I also ate too many of them back in my starving writer days—which may or may not now be over. Their flesh was gray and mushy, and the taste of liver from commercial fish food could be disguised only with Tabasco sauce. I didn't eat them because I liked them, but because they were a free meal.

Will was candid about the fish in the river. He said the smaller ones were more or less right off the stocking truck, while the larger, more brightly colored trout were holdover stockers from the previous year or, in a few cases, even the year before that. These bigger fish were nice and fat, meaning there was either enough wild food in the river to support them or that there was some supplemental feeding going on. I didn't ask which because I didn't know what Will had been told to say and it would have been rude to put him on the spot. I've been to a few upscale places where the management swore their fish subsisted entirely on natural food, only to peek under the tarp in the bed of the river keeper's pickup and find a 25-pound bag of Purina Trout Chow.

Later that day, we met the man who was in charge of what was called "the fishing program" at the ranch. He asked how we did in a way that suggested the question was a formality. We said we caught a bunch of nice big trout on dry flies and had a fine day. He smiled slyly and looked down at the toes of his boots as native westerners do when they're about to tell the unvarnished truth. He said, "Well, catchin' fish here is kind'a like gettin' laid in a whorehouse."

Will had alluded to the same thing that afternoon, though not in so many words. When Doug asked him if he ever fished the ranch on his own time, he said no, he preferred to catch wilder fish on public water. I said, "Me, too," and meant it, but under the circumstances it must have sounded a little hollow.

Will also told us that once, when a group of potential home-buyers with deep pockets was scheduled to be shown around the ranch, they'd dumped an extra $50,000 worth of big trout in the river. Likewise, I'm told that when a real estate agent is showing expensive condos in Los Angeles, he'll sometimes hire half a dozen B-list starlets in bikinis to lounge around the pool for the afternoon. Not so much to misrepresent the place, you understand, as just to create a certain ambience. The sales tactic is as old as the hills because it works. An extremely sharp cookie carefully considers price, terms, location, and return on his investment, then reveals his fundamental humanity by tumbling for some high-end tits and ass.

I really do prefer wild trout in public water, but I know a little something about these upscale places because I've fished them off and on for years. Once—so long ago now it seems like another life—I'd sometimes go at night out of necessity. More recently, I've been an invited guest. The big dumb trout were always fun, but the real draw was a chance to see how the other half lives, which for most of us is a matter of at least idle curiosity.

As it turns out, it's actually rare for these folks to be

boardroom tyrants to whom catching a trout is the sporting equivalent of a hostile takeover, although there are just enough of those to generate the stereotype. In my experience, most of the people you meet at these places are earnest, but not very good fly fishers, with few surviving illusions and a unique set of problems. It's widely assumed that small money is earned, while big money is ill gotten, but it's rarely that simple on either count. It's also a common belief that if you ever had enough money, you'd never worry about money again, but in reality, the more you have, the more you fret.

It was a revelation and a comfort to learn that wealth hadn't always made these people as happy as they'd assumed it would. Someone once said, "It costs a lot to be rich," and that can turn into a vicious, escalating spiral with no end in sight as the well-off try to isolate themselves from the simultaneous envy and enmity of the lower classes. This can reach lynch-mob proportions in hard economic times when even the densest among us come to realize that the flip side of "too big to fail" is "too small to matter."

There can also be a fragility to riches that isn't evident to outsiders, since wealth is now measured more by flimsy paper than by actual bars of gold in a vault. Warren Buffett once said, "Until the tide goes out, you don't know who's been swimming naked." A Chinese proverb says, "When the river is high, the fish eat the ants; when the river is low, the ants eat the fish," which the ants would tell you is exactly what they deserve.

But back to the point, which was fishing. A well-heeled late friend of mine once told me, a little ruefully, that when it comes to fly fishing, money can buy you everything you want except the time it takes to become a good fisherman. I've since learned that this is a common problem. People rarely come right out and admit it, but after an hour or two on the water it becomes obvious.

At the time, this guy had gotten very comfortable, as they say, doing something I didn't understand with other people's money. But then as sometimes happens, his deal went south, the Securities and Exchange Commission called, and rather than face the music, he killed himself with an expensive English shotgun.

But before his troubles, he was a surprisingly normal and generous friend whose only apparent flaw was that he happened to be wound a little too tight. I suppose we were an odd couple from opposite sides of the tracks, but we got along well in spite of having nothing much to talk about except fly fishing—or maybe because of that, now that I think about it. To this day, I couldn't say how well I actually knew him. All I know is that the news of his suicide was a shock but not quite a surprise.

If he'd lived and prospered, I'm sure he'd have eventually bought a multimillion-dollar summer place on one of these "ranches" where he'd have vacationed with his fourth wife. (He was on his third when he died.) He'd have had me up for a boys' weekend every late summer or fall when the fishing was good and the wife was away. He'd have secretly considered the invitation to be an act of charity, and I'd have just as secretly forgiven him for that—feeling a little superior in the process. We'd have eaten well, talked about the old days, and caught large stocked trout without too much effort. It wouldn't have made me feel like the Pathfinder in a James Fenimore Cooper novel, but it would have been fun.

16

A GOOD YEAR

It dawned on me only gradually how good the fishing was that late summer. I was doing well, but at first I assumed it was luck, which you learn to accept without question because you can jinx a good streak with second thoughts. Then, when it went on longer than luck usually lasts, I thought it must be persistence. I was catching lots of trout, but I was fishing almost daily: two things that naturally go together. Then I decided that after all these years I was just getting to be a damned fine fly fisherman and modestly resolved not to lord it over anglers who weren't as skilled as I was.

This, as you may know, is how fishermen think, so it was only through the usual process of elimination that it could finally sink in: This had nothing to do with me except that I was there to see it. The fishing had simply been as good as I could remember in thirty-five consecutive seasons on the same water.

It was with that in mind that I took a friend from Minnesota to one of my favorite parts of the upper drainage in mid-September, at the tail end of the all-too-short high-country season. As we hiked back to my pickup at the end of the first day, he said, "This is some of the best small-stream trout fishing I've ever seen," and I don't think he was just being polite. I'd been about to say the peak had passed and it had actually slowed down some over the last two weeks but then decided to keep my mouth shut. Or at least that's what I think now, although I often remember myself being more inscrutably silent than I really was.

The friend was sporting artist Bob White, and he eventually did an oil painting based on photos he took on that trip. It depicts me just recognizably in the near distance fishing a favorite pool on my favorite stream toward the bittersweet end of a benchmark season. I now have a print of the painting hanging as prominently as possible in my house. Half a dozen people have admired it for a minute or two before turning to me and saying, "Dude, that's you!"

It was in early July of that same year that Jeff Pill called. Jeff is a TV producer with a soft spot for fishing videos, and he asked me to be part of a documentary he was doing for the American Museum of Fly Fishing. It would show fly fishers whose names you might know explaining why they fish and then in most cases actually fishing, as if to prove they weren't just talking a good game. He wanted to film my segment on my home water, and for mysterious production reasons, this would have to happen in mid-July or not at all.

I explained that we'd had an unusually heavy snow pack in the mountains, the water was still high, and the local creeks probably wouldn't drop enough to fish well until early August. He said he was sure we could work something out, which I understood to mean that *I* would have to work something out.

I went at this backward, which is the first sign that I'm in over my head. First, I told Jeff I'd be in the video on his strict schedule. Then I drove up to the creeks to see if it would be possible to catch a trout on anything classier than a gob of worms.

I stuck to the lower, roadside stretches of two nearby streams. The prettiest and best fishing is higher up the drainage, but the water up there would still be too cold to fish well and too hard to get to for the purpose of shooting the video. Jeff had said anyplace we filmed would have to be pretty easily accessible. There'd be a crew of four with cables, reflectors, and such to lug around, plus bulky sound equipment and an equally large, heavy camera. Also the cameraman, Bob Hanna, was still recovering from a badly broken leg. He was hobbling along valiantly and without complaint, but we'd have to go easy on him.

I thought the fishing was a little marginal for show business. The weather had turned hot, but all that did was melt more snow in the high country, so the streams swelled up and the water temperature dropped as the air temperature rose. There weren't many insects hatching yet, and the higher flow in the last of the runoff didn't leave much holding water, so catchable fish were far between. I found that a diligent small-stream fisherman could hook the odd trout, but it took time and he had to cover lots of water, while we'd be on a tight schedule and were limited to a handful of pools within sight of convenient turnouts.

When the day came, I couldn't buy a strike in camera range in two or three pools, and things were beginning to look desperate. But then in another run, I managed to nick and miss two trout that might have gone nine inches and land a much smaller brown. Actually, it was a cute little baby trout still in parr marks: a fish so tiny I'd have been embarrassed to catch it if I were by myself—and I'd just done it in front of witnesses and on film.

We ended up shooting for three days: on the creek, at my desk at home, and on a private ranch pond where I managed to catch a sixteen-inch rainbow, much to everyone's relief. All in all, it was an interesting if somewhat nerve-wracking experience, and I could never quite forget that fishing has never really worked for me as a spectator sport. Fishing is like sex in that it can be anywhere from deeply meaningful to just plain fun to participate in, but it's oddly boring to watch in videos. Through it all, Jeff kept saying, "Don't worry, this isn't reality, this is television," which I think he meant to be comforting.

By the time the film crew left, my nerves were shot, so I went back to the creek and fished up a half mile of the steepest, gnarliest, least-accessible water in the south canyon. This was the epitome of the kind of place that was out of the question for a cameraman with a bum leg, and I reveled in the freedom to scramble along at will and unobserved. Naturally, I hooked one or two fat brown trout in every slick and eddy where I thought one should be and never missed a strike. "Don't worry," I said to myself out loud, "this isn't television; this is reality."

It was probably significant that the fishing picked up as soon as I was through trying to show off, but if there was a lesson there, I can't say I learned it. I was too busy absorbing the idea that the creeks were fishing well a good two weeks or more before I usually started fishing them and also dealing with my embarrassment that this was such a big surprise.

I've been casting a fly rod on these streams since the end of the Nixon administration and had long since bought into the common belief that we local fishermen know the score better than anyone. But as Robert Traver once pointed out, that belief can make us complacent, which is why a stranger will sometimes show up, unburdened by habits and preconceptions, and fish circles around us.

The problem was, I'd come to know the water well enough to tell at a glance when the conditions were ideal, but I'd gotten spoiled and had fallen into the habit of waiting for that, either traveling other places to fish or moping around home until everything was perfect. I did the obvious calculation. If I'd missed out on two extra weeks every season for the last thirty-five years, that meant I'd moped through almost a year and a half's worth of fishing that I'll never get back. Yikes!

Of course, the creeks were still largely unwadable, and the pools and glides that reveal themselves in lower flows were still mostly white water. From the vantage point of the pickup driving the canyon roads—my usual lazy scouting strategy—the streams didn't look all that inviting. On closer inspection, though, the water was clear enough and the trout were neatly tucked into miniature slicks and eddies, some of which you could pick out only at almost point-blank range.

Sometimes it was impossible to get close enough for the short, high-stick cast it takes to get a drift in fast, conflicting currents, so I caught trout from the places I *could* reach and shrugged off the rest philosophically. It's an odd fact of life that whichever side of a stream you're on, two-thirds of the best water is out of reach on the other side. You're constantly tempted to try to wade across, but although these are small streams by anyone's definition, that doesn't mean people haven't managed to drown in them when the water is high.

It didn't surprise me that the fish were in good shape. Trout feed well in high water, and the longer the runoff lasts, the fatter they get until even the small ones are built like little salmon and the bigger ones put a dangerous bend in a 4-weight fly rod. There did seem to be a lot of fish that year, but at first I thought they were just concentrated in a few spots by the high water. Then as the flow dropped and there were more good places to fish, there still seemed to be trout everywhere.

By early August, it became clear that this was shaping up to be one of those seasons we get maybe once in a decade when everything that *can* go right miraculously does: the exact opposite of Murphy's law. These small, freestone streams reflect not only the current conditions, but also what it's been like for any number of previous years. In the past seven seasons, we'd had five years of relative drought that kept the numbers of fish and the fish themselves on the skinny side. That was followed by two high-water years during which more trout wintered over successfully, two age classes were added to the population, and they all ate like kings during two consecutive high runoffs.

In retrospect, it was as simple as that, and I probably could have foreseen this if I was the kind to make predictions, but I'm not. I just fish, hoping for the best, and when things go well, I assume the gods have smiled. And anyway, my record for predicting the future is so poor that the smart people I know will no longer take my advice.

I spent the better part of six weeks that summer looking over my shoulder, expecting word of the good fishing to get out and the creeks to start filling up with unfamiliar fishermen, but it never happened. Between fly shops, the Internet, and the old low-tech grapevine, there are few secrets left except for those no one cares to know about, but in these days of hog-hole tailwaters and competitive fly fishing, a good season on a handful of mediocre mountain creeks just isn't likely to draw more than the normal crowd. Fish porn is the new ideal, and to be a true creek fisherman you have to see the proletarian charm of trout that neatly fit three abreast in a twelve-inch frying pan.

So I had the streams to myself for a couple of weeks, but as August wore on and water conditions became perfect, the usual contingent began to show up, most of whom I know at least by sight. Some of these people are genuine small-stream aficionados and others are just marking time until they can get somewhere better, but they all know the water and do some serious business. Twenty-five years ago, there might have been eight or ten of these regulars. Now there are probably more like thirty, plus some weekend tourists and local dabblers who don't do much harm. That's still a manageable number on over a hundred miles of water, especially if you avoid fishing on Saturdays and Sundays.

So some days there'd be a familiar pickup parked at a

turnout I had in mind, but there'd always be plenty of vacant creek both upstream and down, and it was all fishing beautifully. Twice glorious days abruptly went dead, and I understood I'd come up behind another fisherman who knew what he was doing. Once I walked upstream, found the guy, and we had a little conference. He said he planned to fish as far as where the first logjam used to be and then head home for dinner. I said I'd hike on up and get in above that. All very civilized.

Another day the same thing happened, but it was already going on five o'clock and I'd caught plenty of fish, so I reeled in and hiked out. Halfway back on the trail, I overtook a woman about my age carrying a spinning rod and asked her how she did. She produced two large plastic bags from her daypack. One held a double handful of wild boletus mushrooms and the other seven keeper-sized brook trout—three over the limit, but who's counting? At first I cringed at the sight of dead trout from "my" creek, then I wished I'd thought to keep a few for myself. That was the most crowded day of the summer.

I naturally wanted to share this information with fishermen I knew and liked (without being too promiscuous about the news), but my friends are now mostly grownups and were too busy to fish almost every day. (If the truth were known, I was, too, but I did it anyway.) So I ended up doing most of my local fishing alone, which I've always liked and have lately come to prefer. I haven't given this a lot of thought, but I suspect it has to do with shedding the tyranny of schedules and sidestepping the hint of competition that creeps in even among the best of friends. There's also something about spending entire days without conversation—not counting the internal dialog we carry on with ourselves through all but the most enlightened hours of every day. Eventually, I begin to realize that too many of the words I speak are just noise designed to fill an awkward vacuum.

Once I've lost it—and it's easy to lose—it can take me days or even weeks of solitary fishing to rediscover the habit of stillness. But eventually the drone of journalism on the car radio as I drive to and from the streams begins to seem inconsequential. First, I'll turn it down until it's muttering almost inaudibly, and then I'll finally just turn the damned thing off—a genuine moral victory for a news junkie. At about that point, I heard from a young Marine I'd been corresponding with. He's home now after doing three tours between Iraq and Afghanistan, and considers himself lucky because the only lasting effect is a case of tinnitus from being too close to too many loud noises. He said, "Fly fishing is the only peace and quiet I get now. The sound of the water over the rocks drowns out the chronic ringing in my ears."

At home I'd do the minimal chores required to stay clean, fed, and solvent and remind myself that if you ignore a ringing telephone it eventually stops. Sometimes I'd tell myself I should work on the book I was supposed to be writing or reset the post for the mailbox, which hadn't been the same since a hormone-crazed teenager bombed it with a jack-o'-lantern the previous Halloween. But then either or both would have cut into the fishing time.

That's not to say it's entirely out of character for me to bag work and go fishing. It's just that, with the streams fishing so well, my usual predisposition went to a whole other level. Jim Harrison once said, "An obvious boon in a writer's life is that he can concentrate his work into the months when no suitable sport is available." Or to put it another way, when the trout are biting, shit-canning the career can seem like a viable option. Some—including my late father and two ex-wives—have suggested that this tendency indicates a lack of ambition, but that's not it. It's just that good fishing doesn't last forever, but the day-to-day reaping and sowing does. They say the idea is to sacrifice your enthusiasms in order to get ahead, but ahead of what?

I long ago came to believe that in the interest of basic mental health, everyone should have a specific obsession firmly in place: some mindless eagerness so compelling it seems to emanate from the universe at large rather than your own hyperactive brain. (And I mean something that won't get you arrested or trigger an intervention.) When you finally lose it, catch yourself yelling back at the television and know you're utterly sunk, that's no time to start wondering if you should take up a hobby.

But I've also learned that there's an art to being unaccountable without ultimately ending up sleeping on a park bench. It involves the rare ability to check out indefinitely while leaving open the very real likelihood that you'll check back in at some point. (Not forgetting that reentry can be a time-consuming shock to the system.)

This quest for an elusive balance is what causes some to turn to self-help books and lifestyle gurus, even though neither is especially helpful. I suspect that Marsha Sinetar's book *Do What You Love, the Money Will Follow* gave a handful of readers a wonderful life and put many others in the poorhouse. When Timothy Leary advised us to "Turn on, tune in, and drop out," it sounded good until you realized it was like telling someone how to sky-dive by saying, "Just jump out of the airplane and hope that the weight you've been feeling on your back is a parachute."

My generation has been especially prone to this kind of foolishness, and I'm not the only one of us who woke up in his early forties—with not much more than a pot to piss in—thinking, Okay, I'm functionally self-aware and I know how to fish. Now what? On the other hand, fishing when the fishing is as good as you've seen it in years can seem like a civic duty. And for that matter, it's comforting to live by your wits in one of the few places left on earth where your wits are sufficient. In the end, you may never get it exactly right—Annie Dillard said, "There is no shortage of good days; it's good lives that are hard to come by"—but it's still worth trying.

The video was released in September, shortly after I took Bob up for some of the last of the good fishing on the creek. Jeff and I sat alone on the deserted back stairs at a fly-fishing show in Denver and watched the final cut—minus the music—on a laptop. I realized I'd had no expectations beyond the secret hope that I wouldn't look or sound stupid, and through the magic of editing, I didn't.

I also saw why it had been necessary to tediously shoot the same things over and over again, pretending it was fresh each time. The idea was to make it look as though three or four cameras covered the action when in fact there was only one. Which is to say, everything that appeared to happen in my short segment actually *did* happen, although not always exactly as it appears on screen. I hope that doesn't give anything away.

17

FOOD

I had one of the best steak dinners of my life on the outskirts of Valentine, Nebraska. It was at a family restaurant called the Bunkhouse, one of those places designed to feed the locals as well as snag passing tourists in season with the usual corny western motif and a "Little Cowpoke Special" on the kids' menu. There were a few paved parking spaces out front, but Ed and I were towing a bass boat, so we drove around back to the enormous dirt lot reserved for campers and eighteen-wheelers.

A hot wind was blowing out of the east across a pasture and a truck stop, and there was dust in the air along with the combined aromas of cow flop and diesel.

We'd been fishing all day over near Ainsworth and just wanted a store-bought meal, air conditioning, and no dress code beyond the usual SHIRT AND SHOES REQUIRED. The alternative would have been to drive the twenty miles back to our rented cabin at Big Alkali Fish Camp, an airless wooden box that would be too hot for cooking until 10 P.M.

We were desperately hungry, and I'm sure that had something to do with it, but the fact is, this was an excellent locally raised rib eye that was cooked to the Platonic ideal of medium rare. That requires exquisite timing, since the marbled fat in beef keeps it cooking for a little while after it's removed from the heat, so if you cook it till it's done, it ends up being *too* done. You tell how ready a steak is by the way it feels when it's wiggled with a fork. A raw steak feels blubbery; a well-done (that is, ruined) steak feels like the sole of a shoe, with infinite gradations in between.

The baked potato and the salad were adequate but nothing special. The dinner roll looked and tasted suspiciously like one of those frozen jobs, but only a snob would quibble over a piece of bread when he's just paid a measly ten dollars for a truly memorable steak. The only drawback was that for the rest of the trip Ed kept calling me "little cowpoke."

I once had an equally good steak at a fancy place in Islamorada in the Florida Keys. I'd been fishing for tarpon and bonefish with a record-producer friend who'd had a good year, and one evening he took me and two other friends out for what he called, in a theatrical tone of voice, "a good meal." The restaurant had a piano player tinkling quietly, linen napkins and tablecloths, waiters in silk shirts, a cool breeze wafting in from the Gulf, and a view of yachts and fishing boats on the water. The dress code was relaxed there, too, since this was a fishing town and visiting sport fishermen are forgiven worse misdemeanors than showing up for dinner in shorts and sandals. The steak was every bit as good as the one in Valentine—but no better—and if I read the bill upside down correctly, the tab came to nearly eight hundred dollars for the four of us, although, to be fair, that *did* include brandy and cigars out on the veranda.

I tried to invoke my populist guilt over a meal costing that much, but couldn't bring it off because I was so far out of my element. The producer had just told me that in his best year he made over ten million dollars but that it wasn't as much as it sounded like because "You wouldn't believe my expenses."

I said, "You're right, I wouldn't."

Why eat steak in a fishing town in the Keys? For variety. The standard drill on that trip was to cruise the docks when we came in from fishing to see what the commercial guys were bringing in. When something looked good, you'd note the name on the truck that was picking it up, go take a shower, and then walk or drive to that restaurant and order "the catch of the day," which in this case was exactly that. With fresh cole slaw, hush puppies, and home made cornbread, it would cost about the same as a Big Mac and fries. We'd split the bill with the record producer, which he thought was charming.

We've become an almost totally homogeneous culture now, with a cuisine ruled mostly by junk-food chains, but some Mom and Pop joints have held out, and it still seems true that if there are cattle grazing within sight of a restaurant, the owners probably know how to cook a steak. The same goes for seafood when you can glance out the window and see fishing boats tied up at the dock. In most towns in northern Wisconsin, you can order the walleye special without checking the menu to see if they have one. In northern Michigan, it's lake whitefish, walleye, or perch. On the other hand, beware of "wild Rocky Mountain trout" on menus in the Mountain West. It's a hatchery fish, or at least it damned well better be, since selling wild game under any circumstances is illegal.

The legitimacy of delivering a stringer of wild trout and a few grouse to a friend who owns a good restaurant and having him cook them for you during regular business hours is a little less clear. You order the Colorado Surf and Turf Special with a conspiratorial wink, but the way I see it, you're paying him for the use of a table, a waiter, condiments, silverware, and his considerable skill in the kitchen, but not for the birds and fish that you brought in yourself. Of course, if Big Brother knew about this, he might see it differently.

I do appreciate good food and I'm sincerely puzzled by why it's so hard to find and sometimes so expensive, especially since it's often no harder to cook a good meal than a bad one. Along the same lines, it also seems odd that so much expensive food is so ordinary. On the other hand, I make a living as a fishing writer, so I travel a lot in remote areas and will more or less happily eat anything rather than go hungry. In fact, I've developed a grudging fondness for a certain brand of convenience store microwave mystery-meat burgers, although they tend to be best after a long hard day on the river and when there's nothing else available.

And then there are the countless café breakfasts prepared

by fry cooks whose work is informed by the knowledge that this is the best job they'll ever have. When the plump waitress asks, "How's them eggs?" I smile and say, "They're just like my mom used to make." In truth, they suck, but why begin a beautiful day by being snotty? Meanwhile, a man in the booth behind me whistles tunelessly until his friend says, "Bill, I wish you'd either learn a song or shut the hell up."

I actually go to rural cafés as much for the overheard conversation as for the food. For instance, a regular walks in, the waitress asks if he wants the usual, and he says, "Naw, my wife said she'd leave me if I don't change, so I'm gonna have pumpernickel French toast." Another time a tourist couldn't open the front door, which was swollen and stuck from humidity. She gave up after one try, got back in her car, and drove away. The cook said, "Well, if she can't work the door, she's probably too fuckin' dumb to eat anyway."

Even when I pack my own food, I tend toward the easy, careless meals men eat when they're camping. Once, Susan looked askance at my provisions for a trip. I said, "I know, but I only eat like this when I'm fishing." She said, "Yeah, but you fish *all the time*."

One of my friend A.K.'s favorite camp meals consists of a can of Dinty Moore beef stew sprinkled liberally with garlic salt and served over slices of whole wheat bread (for the fiber to keep you regular). You might briefly wonder about that plug of orange fat that always congeals under the lid, but after a long, cold day of fishing, it tastes great. A friend who once spent time living at an Arctic research station said they'd melt a whole stick of butter in everything they ate and they stayed warm and never gained an ounce. "Good food" is a relative term, and we only start going to fat when we eat like lumberjacks and work as accountants.

Some of the best meals I've had, I've cooked myself, although that's obviously a subjective judgment as well as a selective memory, since some of the worst fall into the same category. Like all middle-aged men who hunt and fish, I feel I have this instinctive knack with wild game, even though there's no big trick to it. When you start with fresh, wild, organic food and a good appetite, all you have to do is not screw it up by overcooking or overseasoning. It goes without saying that you should avoid recipes designed to disguise the taste of wild game. If you didn't want to eat it, you shouldn't have killed it.

There should also be no negative thinking about ingredients. Eat reasonable portions, stay active, and understand that wild food is always better than tame and that there are no substitutes for things like butter, bacon, lard, and salt pork. I should probably admit here that I was traumatized by so-called "health food" back in the 1960s. I came to know it as gummy brown rice, vegetables steamed to mush, loaves of bread heavy enough to double as doorstops, and of course tofu, which a friend says is really just dried latex paint.

On a fishing trip to Hog Park in Wyoming one summer, I grilled venison tenderloin chops for my friend Vince. The meat was from a plump young doe shot the previous fall, and it was untouched by marinade, sauce, or even salt and pepper; just flopped on my folding grill and cooked briefly over pine coals to medium rare—the only proper way to do game. It was so good Vince decided I was a great cook and believes it to this day.

Two days earlier, we'd bypassed an official Forest Service campground and had camped up a four-wheel-drive track along a small brook-trout creek, but that afternoon a bunch of young guys moved in nearby and immediately began blaring a battery-operated boom box and tearing up the landscape on whiny little Japanese dirt bikes. It was too late in the day to break camp, so we decided to gut it out and move in the morning. The venison chops were a soul-saving meal that short-circuited a bad mood, and the next morning, while searching for peace and quiet, we stumbled on a pretty little tributary full of dumb, hungry trout and moved in like we owned the place—which in a way we did.

For some reason, we never ate any trout on that trip, although we could have since we caught plenty and there were no special regulations to prevent it. It's just that catch-and-release fishing eventually becomes so habitual that on most days killing a few doesn't even occur to you. This is a huge change from the days when bringing home a stringer of fish for dinner was the only way wives and mothers knew you hadn't been out drinking.

Often when I do kill and eat wild fish more or less on the spot, I'm so pleased with myself that I swear I'll do it more often, but then in practice it's usually someone else who thinks of it. At a fish camp in the Northwest Territories back in the 1970s, I was happy enough with sandwiches until we got into some small lake trout on streamers one day and the guide suggested a shore lunch. We had steaks cut from a six-pound lake trout fried in bacon fat, canned pork and beans, thick slices of buttered homemade bread, and boiled coffee with condensed milk, all on a bright day that was still chilly enough that it felt good to sit close to the fire.

I recalled that lunch so fondly that the following year I reproduced it over a fire pit at home with a small laker from a nearby reservoir. It was okay, but nothing like I remembered, even though all that was missing was a million-plus square kilometers of northern wilderness straddling the Arctic Circle where, just a week before, the unsuccessful search for a lost float plane had finally been called off. In a place where you could easily wander off and never be seen or heard from again, life seems more precarious than usual and even the simplest meal becomes a banquet.

Most of my meals of fish—and all of the best—have been cooked and eaten within sight of the water where the fish were caught. On a river in Alaska, our guide wordlessly took a lovely four-pound Arctic char I'd just landed and walked up the bank to clean it. I kept casting and never took my eyes off the water, but I heard a driftwood fire snapping behind me on the bank and, a little while later, I smelled fish and assumed that any hungry brown bear within a mile or so downwind could smell it, too.

The char was prepared with what the guide called his "secret recipe": grilled with butter, garlic, and a squeeze of lemon. I'm not being coy when I say I don't remember the name of the river—it was something in Yup'ik with seven or eight syllables—but I remember we'd seen a lynx and a wolverine before noon, and I remember that fish vividly, both in the water and later on a paper plate next to a pile of macaroni salad.

Hunger and wildness are both good sauces for fresh fish and so is blamelessness. When you're with a professional guide who says it's okay to take a fish, you assume it is, if only because guides tend to be insanely protective of the fisheries that provide their livelihoods. It also helps when you've seen hundreds of fish in the last few hours and have caught and released dozens of them (not forgetting that well-meaning people have been wrong before about the unlimited bounty of wilderness).

We do have to think seriously about conservation now, although it's chilling to realize there are catch-and-release fishermen alive today who don't know how to clean and fry a fish. It's one of those good news/bad news deals: a necessary path to a sustainable future versus ancient, but still useful knowledge lost. But for the time being at least, keeping a few fish to eat in places where the regulations allow it doesn't have to be a huge ethical dilemma. For that matter, killing something beautiful, elusive, and delicious and then eating it right on the spot is the kind of pure animal pleasure we all deserve from time to time. Still, I like to eat trout occasionally from home water that I'm intimately familiar with and where if I thought it would do any harm, I wouldn't do it out of pure self-interest. I'm less likely to kill fish on someone else's home water unless I'm invited to.

For instance, there were those brook trout at a private lake where some friends and I were guests. The club wanted to thin out the smaller twelve-to-fourteen-inch brookies, so we had meals of them three nights in a row, cooked three different ways for variety. I wondered about the wisdom of killing so many nice-sized brook trout, but the club had a management plan, and who was I to argue? In the end, it was a rare, decadent treat of my favorite fish.

There was the little three- or four-pound jack salmon I caught in another river in Alaska that took the 3/0 hook too deep and came in streaming blood from his gills. He was dead anyway—the angling equivalent of roadkill—so we delivered him to Patty Kent, the outfitter's wife, who baked him and served him on a platter with carrots and potatoes.

On a fly-out for Arctic char in Labrador, Pierre, our pilot, made a version of seviche. He chunked up the fillets from several big char and put them in a covered plastic tub with lemon juice, olive oil, onions, and garlic. He then slipped it under one of the seats in the de Havilland Beaver, where the bumpy three-hour flight back to camp automatically stirred the marinade. Then we ate it all on Ritz crackers and almost ruined our dinner.

And there was the mess of brown trout we cooked up one late September evening after a landowner on the stream asked us to kill some so they wouldn't overpopulate and stunt. We butterfly-filleted six or eight small trout and spread them out on a wire grill. It was after dark, and you could clearly see the glow of the hardwood coals through their flesh, silhouetting the bones and spots like an edible stained-glass window. Browns aren't usually my favorite trout to eat, but these tasted the way food always does when you're simply alive and therefore hungry.

18

BLUE-WINGED OLIVES

For most of a decade, I refused to bring a fly rod on the annual elk hunt. That's because my friends Ed, DeWitt Daggett, and I hunt too conveniently in the headwaters of the Frying Pan River in western Colorado, about a forty-minute drive upstream from the Gold Medal water below Ruedi Dam. We're there in mid-October when the Blue-winged Olive mayfly hatch can be on, and back when I used to bring one, having a fly rod along created a needless distraction. In years when the hunting was slow, I could get to thinking about fishing, and although I never actually *went* fishing before we'd put in the meat, the nagging possibility had a way of disturbing my fragile concentration.

But then last season, we had one of those charmed hunts. DeWitt and I each had an elk down by noon on opening day, and by dark the following evening we had them both skinned, quartered, packed out, and hanging in the shed at the cabin to age. The next afternoon, with time on my hands and nothing better to do, I drove down to look at the river.

It was a chilly day with a falling barometer, no wind, and a dark overcast that made the sky look ten feet overhead: the kind of textbook Blue-winged Olive day you can wait weeks for. There were only a few fishermen on the water, and in every likely place I looked, Blue-winged Olive mayflies were hatching and trout were eating them, including a brown I spotted in a backwater that would have gone eighteen inches.

Not having a rod with me wasn't as frustrating as you'd think. The hard work of packing two elk out of the mountains in a day and a half had temporarily taken the edge off my sporting ambitions, so for once it was enough just to stand there and enjoy the hatch for the pretty sight it was.

Those rising trout didn't exactly haunt me all the following year, but when I was packing for this fall's hunt, I threw in a rod, reel, waders, and vest without a second thought. I wasn't so much breaking a self-imposed rule (which I reserve the right to do, by the way) as betting that I'd finally matured enough over the last ten years to keep my mind on one thing till it was done. You do finally come to realize that you can't do it all and that if you try you'll end up driving yourself and others nuts in the process.

Things went differently this year. It took us almost the entire ten-day elk season to get the two animals we need to feed our three households, and the morning we pulled out of camp was the kind of bright, sunny one Blue-winged Olives don't like. I stopped here and there to look at the river on the way out of the valley, but I didn't see a single rise. I could also remember my friend Roy Palm telling me ten days earlier that the hatch had just about petered out for the year, although, as usual, if you looked long enough in the right places and under the right conditions, you couldn't rule out finding a few trout rising to Olives.

There was a long moment of indecision. Stringing up a rod always requires a suspension of disbelief, but with the wrong weather, the river looking dead, and the local guru guessing that the hatch was over, the chances seemed too slim.

On the long drive home, I wondered how I'd managed to miss the beginnings of the Blue-winged Olive hatches back in mid-September. I'm writing this only a few months later, but already I can't remember what I was doing instead. I hope it was important. I think of my life as reasonably exciting, but I have to admit that some of my days are spent just getting up to let the cats in and out.

But then early in October, before the hunt, I'd had two good days on Olive hatches closer to home on the Big Thompson River. The first day was the kind you hope for—gray, chilly, good stream flow, not much wind—and Doug and I picked out a short stretch of the catch-and-release water for no other reason than that there were no cars parked at the nearest turn-out.

There were a few size 18 Olives popping off and a handful of scattered rises when we got on the water a little after noon, but over the next few hours it gradually built to a full-blown hatch.

At the height of it, there were dozens of trout feeding within range at any given moment—enough that you had to resist the temptation to flock-shoot and pick out a single fish to cast to. We caught trout in fits and starts from about one o'clock till four, with the usual few minutes of confusion when the size 18 flies were seamlessly replaced by size 22s. In my experience, the trout always notice that before the fishermen do.

Enough said. The best fishing yarns always have to do with unlikely successes or spectacular failures. When you just hit the hatch dead on, have the right flies and catch fish, there's not much more to say.

Two days later, I went back by myself. It was supposed to have been another calm, cloudy afternoon, but the sky was clear blue and sunny, and there was the kind of stiff westerly breeze that warns of an approaching front and also makes casting real annoying. I went to the same place for the same reason (no other cars at the turn-out) and found just a smattering of size 22 Olives petering off below the riffles: the kind of short, halfhearted emergence you often see when the hatch is on but the weather is off. There were a few dinks rising sporadically out in the main current, while the bigger trout were tucked into eddies along the rip-rapped far bank where they could sip stray duns without working too hard.

I waded as close as I could get and tried for a downstream slack line cast. Even at close range, mending a 4-weight line in the wind was tricky, but I did get enough good drifts to hook a handful of fish—maybe six or seven—and managed to land all but two of them. None were huge, but they were all big enough to have pushed the smaller trout out of the best feeding lies.

A week and a half later, after the elk hunt, I went back to

the Thompson, but while I was gone, they'd cranked up the discharge out of Olympus Dam to white-water proportions, three or four times the normal flow for this small canyon river. I drove the whole roadside catch-and-release stretch looking for fishable water and found one other fisherman who seemed to be having a hard time of it with nymphs and an indicator. When he caught me watching, he shrugged as if to say, "What the hell, it was worth a try." I gave him a sympathetic wave and drove home.

Not long after that, my friend Vince and I towed his drift boat up to the North Platte River in Wyoming for the fall streamer fishing, but late in the day we stumbled on a heavy Blue-winged Olive hatch. We were rigged for streamers with big flies and 8-weight rods, but we anchored out, pawed through our gear, and located a couple of small dry flies.

The Olives hatching that day were size 26s, but the smallest fly we were able to dig up between us was a number 22. (We'd both left our tiniest flies at home in Colorado because we were going streamer fishing.) On the water, the size 22 parachute looked like a tugboat in a fleet of canoes, but a couple of small, overeager trout ate it anyway.

A few days later, Doug and I drove down to the South Platte near the town of Deckers looking for Olives, only to find that they'd bumped the flow a hundred cubic feet per second the night before. The river wasn't too high to fish, but nothing was hatching and the trout were scattered and confused, as they tend to be when water levels jump suddenly. We managed to catch a few on nymphs, and Doug got the only rising trout of the day on an Olive emerger.

A few days later, I heard that, although the Thompson was

still running higher than normal, the flow had been dropped "some" and there were a few Olives coming off, so Vince and I drove up there.

The water was clear, but still deeper and faster than most of us like, as witnessed by the fact that it was a Sunday and we didn't see any other fishermen. We tried it anyway. Vince is a big guy and a strong enough wader to have dragged me bodily across more than one deep, fast river I couldn't wade alone, but I volunteered to stay close to the near bank while he slogged out into the current.

I found a few trout rising in foamy eddies tucked into the overhanging willows along that side. There were some size 24 midges on the water and a smattering of the same-sized Blue-winged Olives, so I tied on a number 24 Olive parachute on the theory that trout have a sweet tooth for these bugs and will pick them out of a crowd.

I was a right-handed caster working up a brushy right bank against a downstream breeze, so it didn't all go smoothly, but I managed to hook four trout and land three of them, including one fourteen-inch brown that peeled into the main current and took me on a pretty good ride.

And so it went through the rest of October and into November. I didn't always find Olives hatching, but when I did, I always managed to catch a few fish, if only because trout really do like these little bugs, so you always start with a leg up. Like most Colorado fly fishers, I tend to do well on these familiar hatches—or at least as well as can be expected under the circumstances—which is naturally better some days than others. The modern depictions of fly fishing in print and video are accurate as far as they go, but they usually run heavy on gratuitous fish catching and light on the long silences that characterize the sport—the only true silences many of us ever experience. On a day-to-day basis, fly fishing seems more like stand-up comedy, of which Steve Martin said that the trick isn't to be great, because if you do it enough, the odds are you'll have the occasional great day; the trick is just to be consistently good.

By mid-November, the rivers still looked inviting (when don't they?), but they were also beginning to get that wintry feel, with leafless trees, crusts of bank ice, and noticeably thinning crowds. At that point, the hatch had been on in one river or another in the region for about two months. Even with a late start, I'd been chasing it off and on for the better part of six weeks and had hit it right exactly once. That seemed like enough and would probably have to be, since the later it got in the year, the less likely it was to happen again, although it still wasn't impossible.

There was a time when mid to late November marked the bitter end of the Olive hatches here, but in recent years Colorado has fallen into a pattern of long, lingering autumns followed by abrupt winters (a likely effect of global warming, they say) and the die-hards have learned that short, unreliable Olive hatches can now last well into December.

These late Olives are often the smallest ones you'll ever see—sizes 24, 26, or even 28. We know that each size represents a different species of mayfly, but most are happy enough to refer to them all by the common name, prefaced by a hook size. Taxonomy aside, the visual impression is that the same flies that started in September are still petering off three months later, but they've shrunk from the same cold that now turns your feet numb and freezes your fly line in the guides. But you keep at it because fishermen are helplessly true to their nature and continue to fish against the odds, although never without hope: an impulse Thomas McGuane described perfectly when he called his 1980 book on sport *An Outside Chance*.

Of course, there's no virtue in fishing and even less in fishing hard into what has begun to look very much like the off-season when it becomes clear that catching fish is the goal of the sport, but not necessarily the point. On slow days, you're more likely to feel heroic than stupid, even though you're not doing anything useful or even just going to work in any way society would recognize. You can't even claim to be honing skills like patience and observation that you'll later use in real life. (Jim Harrison once said that all that time in the wilderness prepares you for is more time in the wilderness.)

This thought can arrive unannounced when you stay till dark on the South Platte, then drive the winding road up through Buffalo Creek and Pine and turn east on Highway 285 into the glare of headlights heading west out of Denver. As I said, there's no virtue to it; this is just who you are.

19

CONEJOS

I was in town on a chilly November afternoon doing some unavoidable errands when I got to thinking about fishing. Daydreaming, actually, which is not the wisest thing to do while driving in traffic. I have enough trouble as it is in town because of sensory overload: There are too many cars, bikes, people, and buildings in too small a space, not to mention all the loud noises, sharp corners, and a creepy absence of wildlife.

To reconnect with reality, I'll sometimes stop at a certain

sidewalk café to feed muffin crumbs to the English sparrows that hang out there, hoping they'll be as happy to see me as I am to see them. I'm told this is frowned upon for health reasons, although it's not clear if they mean the health of the customers or the sparrows.

Once, while sitting in the parking lot of a McDonald's in Boulder, I started feeding a few sparrows, and by the time I ran out of fries, my truck was surrounded by sparrows, starlings, a few grackles, a small flock of crows, two ravens, and several herring gulls from a nearby reservoir. I don't think I actually scared away any customers, but I did get some funny looks and no one parked anywhere near me.

Anyway, it was somewhere between the supermarket and the hardware store that I involuntarily visualized a trout stream I'd fished two years earlier high up in the San Juan Mountains in southern Colorado. I could clearly see a size 16 parachute dry fly drifting perfectly down an idyllic pool below a small waterfall. (Accurately recalling an entire day of fishing is like trying to put smoke back down a chimney, so you settle on these specific moments.) When a fifteen-inch cutthroat calmly ate the fly, I realized I'd driven six blocks in a trance and had missed my turn. If I'd hit anything, I probably would have noticed, but it occurred to me that fishing reveries are at least as serious a driving hazard as cell phones.

The stream in this recurring daydream was one Vince and I fished two years ago with Jon Harp, who guides on the Conejos River drainage in that part of southern Colorado that was once part of Mexico. (This would once have been known as the Río Conejos, or River of Rabbits—don't ask me why.) We were there because when I'd met Jon at a fly-fishing show in Denver seven months earlier, he'd generously offered to show us around on some of the secret or at least little-known high-country trout streams in this area that he fished and sometimes guided on.

I consider catching wild trout in small mountain creeks to be my modest specialty, even though it amounts to one of the easiest and least glamorous things you can do with a fly rod. There *are* days when catching trout isn't quite as easy as falling off a log, but the real sport is locating the best creeks and then getting yourself there, often on foot through steep, rugged country. So Jon's enthusiasm was believable and infectious and the atmosphere of the show didn't hurt, either. It's no accident that this event is held in January, when spring still seems too far away to offer much beyond theoretical hope and the despondency of the off-season has weakened your sales resistance.

It's also an article of faith in my personal religion that there are countless miles of underfished and underappreciated trout streams in the Rocky Mountain West just waiting for a fisherman with enough poetry in his soul to give them their due. According to official sources, there are 107,403 miles of perennial streams in Colorado alone. Given the nature of mountain drainages and the preponderance of state and federal lands in the West, most of that mileage is small, public, and remote. If you count all the Rocky Mountain States, the number jumps to well over 800,000 miles, and if you follow the continental mountain range north through Alberta and British Columbia, you could be pushing 2 million. How many of those stream miles hold trout in what we'd call "fishable" sizes and numbers is a personal judgment. I know some who'd say not many. *I'd* say more than you think.

Over the last forty years, I've explored one entire drainage from its civilized lower end to the cold cirque lakes and dripping glaciers in its various headwaters, have extensively fished several dozen others, and have casually wet a line in more random creeks than I can remember. A few I discovered on my own—in the way a fisherman can feel he discovered something that was known to be there all along—but most I was shown or told about by those who knew them well.

Every creek fisherman thinks his own small water is the niftiest thing imaginable and they're all right in a way. They've seen more of it than most, know all of its moods, and remember the best vividly. And if some of their claims seem a little over the top, they're still within the normal bounds of hyperbole.

Many of these folks fish their home water alone or with one or two close friends, but their natural secretiveness is sometimes breached by moments of generosity directed at those few they deem worthy. We creek fishermen aren't exactly stingy, but we're as tight-lipped and quietly happy as small animals that have found the perfect hiding place. Creeks are "dear to my heart," as my grandmother would have said, and since I don't have a spare heart to turn to, I'm glad to know there are hundreds of thousands of miles of them: more than I could fish in fifty lifetimes.

I don't know Jon or his situation well, but he struck me as your typical young guy who is now doing fairly well after years of hard apprenticeship in the fishing business—bearing in mind that this is not something you get into for the money alone. It took time and hard work to put it all together, but he now has a small, neat house, a fly shop and guide service, and a few vintage motel units to rent in the tiny town of Mogote on the western side of the San Luis Valley. This is a broad, flat, sparsely populated basin bordered by the Sangre de Cristo and Culebra ranges to the east and the San Juans to the west. The region forms the headwaters of the Conejos, Rio Grande, and Alamosa rivers, and needless to say it's lousy with headwater creeks, some of which still bear their old Spanish names. When I asked him for directions to his place over the phone, Jon said, "If you find Mogote, you can't miss it" and he was right. There isn't much there and Jon's little compound pretty much comprises the business district.

Jon said he'd been shown some of the creeks he fishes by the man he'd once worked for and who eventually sold him the fly shop and cabins, but he's since added to that knowledge on his own in fits and starts. He's told his guides about places that they've never seen for themselves and, without saying it out-right, leaves the impression that he knows more than he's willing to talk about. The day Vince and I showed up in Mogote, Jon's wife said he was out on his dirt bike looking at a mountain lake he was curious about and she directed us to a nearby stretch of the Conejos. When Jon pulled in later, his bike was dented and muddy and he was trying to hide a slight limp, which his wife seemed to notice without comment.

Over the next few days, we learned that Jon is a fast hiker who would have to stop and wait for us every half mile or so. He's also one of those who lets half the air out of his truck tires so he can go faster than most would on rocky four-wheel-drive tracks, never mind that this makes blowouts more likely and cuts the life of your tires in half. The man seems more eager than actually high-strung or impatient, but when you fish with him, there's no dawdling.

Every trip has its own routine and we fell into this one easily.

After breakfast we'd meet Jon at the shop, where he'd be gently micromanaging the day's schedule. Then we'd pile into his truck with his dog, Luke, to drive, then hike, then fish. Luke, a ten-year-old black Lab, had the air about him of a dog who always goes along, so there was no wiggling or fawning. He'd just hop in the back, take up his usual post, and wait patiently.

I asked Jon if Luke had been easy to train (some dogs are) and he said no, he was actually pretty hardheaded at first, but before getting heavy with him he decided to take a few months and just "double the love." That did it.

Jon was free with the names of the streams we fished and understood that we could remember their locations, but he asked us several times to keep quiet about them and we said we would. I think he knew that guiding on so-called secret water would be a losing battle in the end, but he may not have foreseen the exact shape of the problem in the beginning. He said he'd once guided a fishing writer who promised to be discreet, but who then published a detailed list of creeks in a magazine article. And there was the client he'd taken to a certain stream after exacting a vow of secrecy, but the guy had a GPS unit hidden in his pack and when he got home, he published the stream's exact coordinates on his blog.

The meaning of life is found in nothing loftier than what you do every day, and many of Jon's clients would say he's living the dream by hiking daily into remote trout streams, with or without clients, but always with his dog at his heels. He probably is and he clearly adores going fishing, but he may also have begun to realize that turning something you love into a livelihood isn't always a bed of roses, although it *is* a notch or two above the usual drudgery.

Vince and I stayed in one of the kitchenette motel units Jon rents out, but at the end of the day we'd come in bone-tired and too hungry to cook, so we'd drive directly to a great Mexican restaurant just five miles up the road in Antonito. This place is inexplicably called the Dutch Mill, and it was so good we were trying to systematically eat our way through the entire menu from burritos and carne asada to tamales. Then we'd go back to the kitchen table in our unit to plot out where we'd been that day on our own maps for future reference. (Promising not to tell anyone about these creeks doesn't preclude coming back on your own.)

I was using my DeLorme *Colorado Atlas & Gazetteer,* an invaluable large format book of 103 topographical maps covering the entire state in fairly minute detail. Everyone I know has one of these and in theory they'd be interchangeable, but I've written my name on mine with a black Sharpie because by now it contains quite a few notes that shouldn't fall into the wrong hands.

The motel unit itself was straight out of the 1950s, complete with knotty-pine paneling and what could have been the original pots, pans, dishes, and furniture. It was exactly like the first places I stayed away from home on fishing and hunting trips with my father. This was when I was just old enough to have realized I couldn't grow up to be a cowboy after all, if only because cowboys as I understood them from John Wayne movies no longer existed. On the other hand, I was still holding out for something like fur trapper in the Yukon or maybe lion-hunting guide in Africa, inevitably with a beautiful woman and a good dog for company. Being a fishing writer either hadn't occurred to me yet, or it had, but it didn't seem heroic enough.

Many years later, I began to wonder how much of my life now is just the adult version of those childhood fantasies. Of course, the obvious answer is, All the good parts.

It has been two years now, but the streams we fished still haven't run together in memory and may never. Most of these mountain creeks are so similar that if you can fish one well, you can probably fish them all, but they're still as unique as human faces. They all have roughly the same configuration, but if you ever see one that looks almost exactly like another, the effect is eerie.

All the places we fished involved some long, steep hikes—which, as much as anything, was their secret—although some were definitely harder to get to than others. I can still do these long walks at altitude, although they now take me longer than they used to and I have to stop to rest a little more often. But I haven't complained about that since I was in Mexico not long ago reminiscing with a wheelchair-bound expatriate from Colorado about some mountain creeks we both knew about and that he used to fish before his motorcycle accident. I said they were harder for me to get to now, and he replied, a little wistfully, "Well, at least you still got two good legs stickin' out yer ass."

I'll spare you the blow-by-blow account of every stream we fished and I won't say which I thought were the best. That would be pointless and probably rude, since I can't tell you where any of them are. I also won't say which of us caught the most and biggest fish because I'm not interested in competition—and not just because I usually lose—but we did have a couple of favorites.

We fished one on a day when Jon was too busy to come with us. We were looking over the map the evening before and asked about a stream with a long meadow section on it at an elevation of about 10,000 feet. We perked up when Jon said no one he knew had fished it in recent memory. Most of the stream was public, but the access was blocked off at the bottom by a large ranch, the owner of which wouldn't let fishermen through. As a rule, that is. Jon said the one person he did let through once was an especially pretty woman fly fisher. For the rest of us, the only way in was to hike several miles up and around the ranch roughly following the fence line, and then to drop back down to the creek on Forest Service land. Jon added that if we decided to fish it, he'd sure be interested to hear what we found.

It was a fairly grueling walk, but after an hour and a half and hundreds of feet of altitude first gained and then lost, we cut the creek at a steep stretch so brush-choked that it was all but unfishable. We got some nice cutthroats in the few places where we could snake in a cast, but the trout in most of this mile or so will never see a fly that isn't real—an oddly comforting thought for a fisherman.

A little farther on, we topped out into a long high meadow. It was covered with knee-high shrubby cinquefoil in full yellow bloom and dotted with patches of bright purple gentian. The creek meandered through this vegetation for miles, mostly in shallow, fishless riffles, but there were also deep bend pools with waving mats of milfoil and a fat, gullible cutthroat or two between nine and thirteen inches in each one.

When it was all said and done, we guessed the hike at close to ten miles round-trip, and we didn't even make it to the head of the valley where, according to the map, the stream originated at a small mountain lake. That night, after plates of beef enchiladas, we reported to Jon that it was drop-dead beautiful and a lot of fun to fish, but probably not good for clients who think they should get extra inches on their trout for every mile they have to walk.

Another favorite was one I'd call the best if I were one to rate trout streams by size and number of fish. It was another long hike in, first on a faint footpath, then on convenient game trails, and finally cutting cross-country down into a shallow but steep little canyon. It was uncanny to find so many big cut-throats in a stream above 11,000 feet, where many headwaters begin to peter out, but this one carried a good head of clear, cold snowmelt water and had lots of deep pools where the trout could winter over.

This is where I caught the fifteen-inch cutthroat that still haunts my habitual daydreams. It wasn't the biggest fish I got that day, but it was one of the prettiest. It came from the last pool we fished before the long hike out, and the take was so visual that I've since polished the mental image like a worry stone, right down to the sight of Luke wagging his tail when I set the hook.

I should say here that Luke turned out to be one of the great fishing dogs. He always stayed with the people, knew not to get in the water without express permission, and lagged well behind the fishermen, where he'd either watch or doze, depending on his mood. He didn't actually beg when we stopped for lunch, but he let it be known in a dignified way that he'd accept a handout. At the end of the day, when everyone reeled in and he could tell from the body language that we were through fishing, he'd confidently approach with a stick for the fifteen minutes of aquatic fetch that he'd earned by being a good dog.

As Jon threw a stick for Luke in the last pool we fished on

that creek, he turned to me and asked, "So, is this the best cutthroat trout stream you've ever fished?" I began to run through all the cutthroat creeks I know—there have been a lot of them and some were pretty damned good—but then realized it wasn't that kind of question. This was more like a mother who asks, "Isn't this the cutest baby you've ever seen?" Whether it is or it isn't, you'd have to be a complete cad to say anything but "Yes."

20

THREE RIVERS

It was our last full day in Labrador when Robin Reeve, owner of
Three Rivers Lodge, where we'd been staying, asked my fishing
partner C. D. Clarke and me if we minded doing a little walking
to look for brook trout. We said, "Of course not," understanding that at some camps "a little walking" means a little walking,
while at others it's a euphemism for a death march.

It turned out to be fairly easy as backcountry hikes go.
We motored across the lake, left the boat at the mouth of a

medium-sized river, and hiked upstream for an hour through open spruce forest. I had it easiest with just my daypack, a fly rod, and a gas can. C.D.—a sporting artist of some note—had a larger, heavier pack containing not only his fishing and foul-weather gear, but also his painting supplies, including a small homemade portable easel. Our guide, Jordan Locke, outpaced us both with an outboard motor slung casually over his shoulder.

There was no path, but a welter of caribou trails went in roughly the right direction, and when the one you were on started to veer off course, you could just cut a few yards over to another, always keeping the faint sound of the river off your left shoulder. In most places, the ground was matted with slippery caribou moss, so you wanted to move along quickly to make time but also had to watch your footing in the uneven terrain. At one point, I glanced back and thought C.D. had taken a fall, but when I started back to help, I saw that he was just on his hands and knees grazing on low-bush blueberries.

Jordan walked right to the fiberglass canoe that was stashed at the outlet of the next lake. (What they call "rivers" here usually consist of chains of lakes strung together by short rapids.) Since the last time it had been used, a curious black bear had chewed on the canoe a little to see if it was good to eat but hadn't done any serious damage. There were only a few small tooth marks below the water line, and we figured we could keep up with the leaks with the bailing can—a cut-off plastic milk jug—assuming we could find it. After a short search, it turned up fifty yards back in the woods where a playful fisher or marten had nibbled on it, but again, there was no serious damage.

The paddles had been left out in the weather for far too long and had begun to ridge and crack, but they were still serviceable. Sometimes porcupines will gnaw wooden tool handles and canoe paddles for the salt left by sweaty hands. I once lost a perfectly good ax handle that way.

Out on the water, the outboard started grudgingly after what I'll guess were nearly forty pulls on the starter cord, only to sputter uncertainly and then cough and quit a hundred yards up the lake. C.D. shrugged and started paddling. I took his lead, grabbed the other paddle, and joined him.

We knew we still had a long way to go, and this was our way of saying we didn't necessarily want to turn back because of engine trouble, although of course that decision would ultimately be up to Jordan. The guide always holds the final authority in these matters, in part because he's legally responsible, but also because, left to their own devices, some clients would quickly become a danger to themselves and others. (You assume that category doesn't include you without forgetting that everyone makes the same assumption.) But Jordan just bailed some lake water from the canoe and then went back to work yanking the starter, muttering not quite under his breath. You know, the kind of things you'd say to a heavy machine you'd just carried on your back for an hour and that then didn't work.

So we made our way haltingly across the second lake, roped the canoe through another set of rapids, and on across the next lake, alternately sputtering along at half speed and then paddling when the motor stalled and Jordan yanked the starter ferociously and repeatedly. C.D. got it into his head that our paddling humiliated the outboard, causing it to finally start again after a few minutes out of embarrassment. Given my extensive knowledge of internal combustion engines, that sounded plausible.

We did stop and fish that second rapids for a little while, but the rest of the time we kept moving. Labrador is the kind of sprawling northern wilderness where the abundance is impressive but often local and seasonal, so it's not at all unusual to go that far looking for brook trout—or anything else, for that matter. Even the migratory woodland caribou are found either in the hundreds or not at all, depending on when and where you look. Back in 1903, an American adventurer named Leonidas Hubbard tried to cross Labrador from west to east, confidently assuming he could live off the land. If he'd made it, he'd have been the first to accomplish the feat, but he died of starvation.

C.D. and I had spent most of the week in a fly-in spike camp on an even more remote river, catching what we both considered to be more than enough big, pretty Arctic char. These beautiful fish have always taken a back seat to brook trout here for no reason I can see, although I have to admit that it took me five trips to the province before I could bring myself to fish for them seriously and exclusively. It turned out to be well worth the effort.

So you could say this trip with Jordan on our final day was our last chance at a big brook trout, but that would imply a desperation I don't think either of us were feeling. We were honestly sated with catching fish, so if there turned out to be brook trout in this place, well and good. If not, it would be one more of those days outside in wild country that make you think fishing isn't a bad habit as bad habits go.

And even if we did find brook trout, we assumed there wouldn't be a lot of them. If you go to the right places in Labrador at the right time of year under the right conditions, chances are good that you'll land a few anywhere between, say, five and eight pounds, but no honest outfitter can brag about the commercial grade catches you'll hear about from some other wilderness regions. Brook trout can live unusually long lives this far north. The big ones are said to weigh roughly a pound for every year of their age and they can live for ten years. But they're a minority fish to begin with, and the largest ones have survived nearly a decade's worth of hardships, including heavy predation from pike and lake trout. In other words, the reason they get so big here is the same reason why there aren't that many of them. It couldn't possibly be any other way.

I knew C.D. would paint that day because he had painted every day the weather allowed and some when I'd have said it didn't. (I have a clear memory of him hunkered in a canoe in the rain at Vezina Rapids on our first afternoon at the lodge, painting under the shelter of the only umbrella I've ever seen in the back country.) He seemed to be equally skillful and passionate about both fishing and painting, and if he secretly preferred one over the other, I don't know how you'd be able to tell. He also seemed to have a covert supply of energy. The day we got back from char camp, he spent several hours painting a lovely portrait of the old de Havilland Beaver we'd just flown in on and then painted the head and shoulders of a large brook trout on the plane's cowling as a favor to the pilot. All this while I was taking a nap.

I don't remember now if we were running under power or paddling when we rounded a point and saw the rapids we'd been heading for, but Jordan beamed as if he'd just pulled a rabbit out of his hat. It was typical of Labrador for us to have traveled several hours by foot and canoe to reach less than two hundred yards of fast water, a third of it a stairstep cascade that was too steep and fast to fish. These rapids were known as Rick's Surprise, named for the guide who had discovered them by accident. They were known to hold large brook trout on a somewhat unpredictable basis.

We spread out along the riffly channel below the cascade, tied on streamers, and immediately started catching lake trout: nice-sized eight-to-twelve-pounders that were as likely as not to take you into the backing in the fast water. There may have been some mild disappointment all around when the first few fish turned out not to be brook trout, but catching one kind of big fish instead of another is not the worst thing that can happen on a fishing trip, and it's hard to pout convincingly when you're running downstream with backing screaming off your reel.

After a while, C.D. walked back to the canoe, traded his fly rod for his easel, paints, and brushes and set up to work. I'd gotten used to this routine over the last week and had idly wondered what the trigger was. Had the light suddenly gotten just right? Had a composition finally suggested itself? Had he just caught enough fish to let him comfortably put the rod away for a while? Or had he suddenly remembered that he was supposed to be working?

It had become standard procedure on this trip to leave C.D. alone while he was painting (not counting the odd surreptitious glance) and then to look at the finished products later. All I can say by way of a critique is that I liked them. They were as scenic as you'd expect considering their subjects, but not exaggerated or cloyingly romantic. There was a plainspoken, journalistic quality that said, "This is it; I don't have to make it any prettier than it already is."

A competent painter *can* make things prettier or otherwise different than they really are if he wants to, and making that decision is part of the job. Otherwise, painting would have died out with the invention of the camera. Beyond that, I can't tell you much. Back in college, I once spent a semester in an aesthetics seminar in which we were supposed to come up with a working definition of "art." All I remember is that "I'll know it when I see it" wasn't rigorous enough and that for six months I couldn't look at a painting without getting a headache.

When you're a lifelong fisherman, sporting art can eventually become so ubiquitous that most of it dissolves into the background clutter like elevator music, and it takes a singular intelligence and sensibility to break the trance. I own a precious handful of paintings and lithographs that did just that: work by Robert K. Abbett, Russell Chatham, Betzy Ekstam, Bob White, C.D. himself, and a few others. The only thing they have in common is that when I saw them I wanted to look at them every day instead of just that once. Which is to say, I don't know much about art, but I know what I like.

So C.D. painted, perched a little too precariously above the roughest stretch of rapids, and I kept fishing. I don't know how many lake trout I landed, but they finally began to fizzle out soon after I got one that Jordan guessed at fourteen pounds. Then Jordan took me above the rapids, where I swung a Bomber through the outlet slick of the next lake and caught two nice brook trout in the three-pound class. They were undeniably sweet fish, but not the elusive monsters we were hoping for.

Back down below the cascade, I started flipping my weighted streamer upstream into a small, deep slick at the edge of the white water and hooked a fish that hit harder and ran faster than anything I'd caught so far. I was perched unsteadily on a rock for the extra reach, and the fish peeled past me heading downstream, looping yards of slack on the water. There was a moment of confusion while I regained control of my line, but by the time I did, the fish had wrapped me around a midstream rock, and as we came up tight on each other, my leader snapped with an audible pop.

Jordan said, "That acted like a big brook trout." He didn't say it to be mean. It was just an observation.

I immediately began replaying the whole thing to see if there was anything I could have done differently. (I've done this hundreds of times with hundreds of lost fish and have never come to any firm conclusions.) The fact is, I've fished all my life, my understanding of the fundamentals is instinctive, and my reflexes are reliable, if not actually catlike, but none of that has kept things from periodically going right in the crapper—and it never will.

Not long after that, C.D. finished working, started fishing again, and immediately caught a great big brook trout. Once the fish was in the net, there was some discussion about its probable weight. The standard formula using length and girth called it at a little over eight pounds, but the fish was inordinately fat and chunky, built more like a largemouth bass than a normal brook trout, and Jordan wanted to call it at nine pounds. C.D. said, "I don't *need* it to be nine pounds if it really isn't," but Jordan stuck to his educated guess and it didn't take all that much arm twisting to bring C.D. around.

As for me, I was simultaneously happy for my friend and so sick with envy I almost blew lunch. You know how it is.

Back at the lodge that night as we packed up for the early flight out the next morning, I got a look at the painting C.D. did that day. It had never occurred to me that I'd be in it, but there I was, in the precise spot where I'd stood for almost an hour catching one lake trout after another, now immortalized as an anonymous figure in a brown hat.

"One of the most—many would say *the* most—enjoyable outdoorsmen writing today."

—*Kirkus Reviews*

Look for John Gierach's other great books

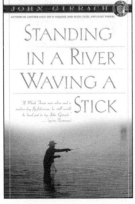